Thomas Hugo

The History of Mynchin Buckland, Priory and Preceptory

In the county of Somerset

Thomas Hugo

The History of Mynchin Buckland, Priory and Preceptory
In the county of Somerset

ISBN/EAN: 9783337164034

Printed in Europe, USA, Canada, Australia, Japan

Cover: Foto ©ninafisch / pixelio.de

More available books at **www.hansebooks.com**

THE
HISTORY
OF
MYNCHIN BUCKLAND
PRIORY AND PRECEPTORY,
IN
THE COUNTY OF SOMERSET.

BY

THOMAS HUGO, M.A., F.S.A., F.R.S.L., &c.,

TRUSTEE AND MEMBER OF THE COUNCIL OF THE LONDON AND
MIDDLESEX ARCHÆOLOGICAL SOCIETY;
HONORARY FELLOW OF THE GENEALOGICAL AND HISTORICAL SOCIETY OF
GREAT BRITAIN;
HONORARY MEMBER OF THE SOMERSETSHIRE ARCHÆOLOGICAL AND
NATURAL HISTORY SOCIETY;
HONORARY MEMBER OF THE SURREY ARCHÆOLOGICAL
SOCIETY;
AND MEMBER OF VARIOUS OTHER LITERARY AND ARCHÆOLOGICAL SOCIETIES.

LONDON:
J. R. SMITH, SOHO SQUARE.
TAUNTON: F. MAY, HIGH STREET.
1861.

PREFACE.

The primary object of the following pages is to furnish the archæologist with as minute an account as can now be recovered of a Religious House of singular interest. Its annals have hitherto been presented to him in a most meagre and fragmentary form, but it has, nevertheless, few equals and fewer superiors in its claims on the attention of every student of our Monastic History, of which, as I have elsewhere remarked, it forms an unique and most instructive chapter.

The account of the place itself, however, includes the mention of numerous details illustrative of Conventual History in general, and of the peculiariatics of the Order of S. John of Jerusalem in particular. Among the former may be noticed the modes of conveying landed and other property to Religious Communities, the burdens by which most of the greater Monasteries were oppressed during the last few years of their existence, and the process by which, after the Dissolution, their possessions were transferred to the King's grantees. And among the latter may be instanced the system and form of Government of the Order of the Hospital, the succession of its earliest Priors of England, the relation of the provincial English Preceptories to the Head House at Clerkenwell, the annual returns made by the various Preceptors to the Prior and by him to the Grand Master of the Order, and the manner of leasing their estates to the several tenant farmers in the fifteenth and sixteenth centuries.

The documents contained in the Appendix will be found a very valuable addition. Almost all of them are now printed for the first time, while the few which have hitherto been committed to the press are now presented with that accuracy the former lack of which was such as to make their re-publication most desirable. I have given them in their original form, only placing apostrophe commas in the stead of those marks of contraction which the fount of the printer did not supply; and, in the case of one MS., I have occasionally added corrections within brackets, where the text was more than ordinarily corrupt, and the reader was, accordingly, more likely to mistake the sense.

Many of my readers will be surprised, as at a fact very much opposed to modern notions on the subject, when told that the spacious County of Somerset contained but four Religious Houses appropriated to women. In the adjacent County of Devon there were but three, while Cornwall did not possess a single example. Of the four Somersetshire Houses the present volume is devoted to the History of one, and I have made extensive and valuable collections towards doing a similar office for the three others, the history of each of which is deeply interesting.

I have only to add that if any one, into whose hands this or any other volume of mine may come, should have it in his power to favour me with the least additional information on the subjects of these researches, I shall be most thankful for its communication, how valueless and unimportant soever it may appear to him to be. It oftentimes happens that an acquaintance with isolated facts of seeming worthlessness is an aid towards the attainment of the most valuable knowledge; inasmuch as such facts are very frequently not only important in other and more direct ways, but also are found to be connecting links between particulars which previously appeared distant from or without any reference to each other, and thus become elucidations of difficulties which would otherwise be hopelessly obscure.

T. H.

5, *Finsbury Circus,*
Ascension Day, 1861.

CORRIGENDA ET ADDENDA.

Page 10, *note* *, *for* 457b *read* 467b; *note* ‡, *for* IV. *read* VI.
—*P.* 11, *n.* *, *add* MS. Harl. 6968, Cart. p. 19.—*P.* 12, *line* 8, *for* Tunccote *read* Tuncot; *l.* 11, *for* Bremesmore *read* Fremesmoro; *l.* 13, *for* Toustoke *read* Toustok; *l.* 25, *for* Merestone *read* Merestou; *n.* *, *for* m. 9 *read* m. 6, *and add* Rot. Hundred. Edw. I., pp. 70, 94.—*P.* 13, *l.* 20, *for* Henbiry *read* Neubiry.—*P.* 20, *n.* *, *for* ad. 9, d. *read* ad. q. d.—*P.* 23, *l.* 5, *for* messago *read* messuago; *l.* 21, *after* years.* *insert inverted commas.*—*P.* 24, *l.* 2, *after* that *insert* the; *l.* 23, *for* park *read* parish.—*P.* 27, *l.* 9, *for* Priory *read* Proceptory.—*P.* 30, *l.* 2, *for* Prunsloe *read* Pruneslee; *l.* 14, *for* clemosynary *read* eleemosynary.—*P.* 36, *l.* 8, *to* Hawlay *add* or Hawley; *l.* 10, *to* Dawson *add* or Dauson.—*P.* 60, *l.* 6, *after* Milo.* *insert inverted commas.*—*P.* 62, *l.* 15, *after* Bourgchier *insert* , Prioress,—*P.* 74, *l.* 6, *insert* John Samweys, or Samwise, requested to purchase the farm of the manor of Toller, with the rectory of Toller, and Wynforde, on the 23rd of February, 1540. ; *l.* 25, *for* Bucklande *read* Buclande ; *l.* 28, *for* scid *read* said.—*P.* 75, *l.* 13, *to* Stapleheys *add* or Staplehayes; *l.* 14, *to* Riden *add* or Roden.—*P.* 77, *l.* 27, *to* Claveshey *add* or Chalveshey.—*P.* 78, *n.* *, *add* Appendix, No. XXII. ; *n.* †, *remove* Appendix, No. XXII.—*P.* 89, *l.* 19, *for* 𝕷𝖆𝖊𝖘𝖍𝖊 *read* 𝕷𝖆𝖚𝖘𝖍𝖊.—*P.* 92, *l.* 6, *for* he'nt *read* h'ent ; *l.* 33, *for* 155 *read* 153.—*P.* 93, *l.* 18, *for* morabant *read* morabant' ; *l.* 36, *for* Buckland *read* Bukland.—*P.* 99, *l.* 25, *for* Som's' *read* Sum's'.—*P.* 100, *l.* 11, *for* Bromfild *read* Bromfeld : *l.* 13, *for* rac'oe *read* raco'e.—*P.* 102, *l.* 8, *for* Priorisa *read* Priorissa ; *l.* 32, *for* u'ror *read* n'ror'.—*P.* 103, *l.* 25, *for* sequens *read* sequene'.—*P.* 104, *l.* 38, *for* tene' *and* face' *read* ten'e *and* fac'e.

Mynchin Buckland Priory and Preceptory.

AMONG the many delightful roads by which a traveller in the west may reach on all sides the fair town of Taunton, he will find few, if any, more agreeable than that which runs from Borough Bridge to the village of Durston, and then, with West Monkton at a short distance on the right and Creech S. Michael on the left, leads him through our favorite Bathpool, and by its picturesque mills, either along the ancient highway, commonly called Old Bathpool Lane, under Creechbury Hill, or by the windings of the Tone and the Priory Fields, to the busy streets and the consequent termination of his journey. He will not have advanced far on the route that I have here laid down, when the matchless vale of Taunton Dean, with its churches and steeples, its mansions and parks, its corn-fields and groves, and its noble framework of Neroche and Blackdown, above the sunny shoulders of Thornfalcon and Stoke, of Orchard and Pickeridge, opens wide before him, and he only relinquishes the charms of the more distant prospect for the shady lanes, the luxuriant vegetation, the tall trees, the lovely river, and the snugly sheltered homesteads, of which his descent into the lowlands soon gratifies him with the closer view. After passing the hamlet of West Ling, and when he is within half a mile from Durston, he may observe in a meadow on his right hand some curious inequalities of the surface, contracting and expanding with that certain definiteness and regularity of outline which assures him of the presence of design on the part of the constructors, though it is more than likely that he may be unable to offer an explanation of the intention which not the less certainly actuated them in their labours. On his left, at the distance of a field from the road, is a modern mansion, and adjoining to it are some agricultural buildings and court and garden walls of an earlier age. These last are the only features which the place now presents of occupation more ancient than his own, save the roads and hedgerows that may have been there for centuries.

Quiet, and still, and lonely is the present aspect of the spot, and yet it was once a scene both of contemplative privacy and of active industry; and they who owned and occupied it were members of a Community that had a long and singular history, and bore a distinguished part in the great world of men and of things. It was the site of the Priory and Preceptory of Buckland, Mynchin Buckland, or Buckland Sororum, one of the Commandries of the Order of S. John of Jerusalem. It was the focus of an influence sensibly and deeply and widely felt. A few crumbling fragments, now recognized with difficulty, once formed the boundary between it and the surrounding world. And the green undulations which attracted our traveller's notice were long centuries ago the demesne Ponds that supplied with their habitual and constant diet the successive Brethren and Sisters of the House.

It is to this very interesting Community that I am about to direct the attention of my reader. And in presenting him with a history of Buckland Priory, I may remind him that I am introducing him to an entirely new and different aspect of Monastic Life and Conventual Usage from those with which I have in previous pages endeavoured to make him familiar. The system of the Hospital itself was unlike all others save one, as I shall presently attempt to show. And, in addition to this, it is specially to be noted that we have here a feature which even in that Order was not elsewhere to be seen in England. Mynchin Buckland was both a Priory and a Preceptory. The latter was a normal example of a Hospitalars' Commandry; the former was the sole instance in the kingdom of its peculiar class. It was a Community of Women, and the only one that the Order possessed. As such, its history presents us not only with a subject of the greatest local interest, but with an unique chapter in monastic annals at large. It is at once a new scene to the student of olden days, and one of which no county but Somersetshire can furnish him with an example.

Before I enter into the vicissitudes of this attractive place, it will be necessary to give my reader a brief outline of the Order to which it belonged. We should otherwise be likely to meet with obscurities in the story which a few words of previous explanation would avail to prevent.

The Order of Knights Hospitalars began and took its name from a Hospital founded at Jerusalem, and its chief objects were the defence of the pilgrims on their road thither, and the care and maintenance of them during their sojourn. It included among its members both men and women; and, of the duties just enumerated, the latter was necessarily as well as specially the office of the Sisters, as was the former of the Brethren. The Knights, or officers of the highest rank, were called in the first instance Knights of S. John of Jerusalem; and afterwards, from the place of their successive residence, Knights of Rhodes and Knights of Malta. The Hospital was founded in the Holy City about the year 1092, and was dedicated to S. John the Baptist. Eight years afterwards the Order was introduced into England, and the brethren's first house was built for them at Clerkenwell in the year 1100. They soon acquired immense wealth, which was much increased in the earlier part of the fourteenth century by the cession to them of the estates of the suppressed Order of the Knights Templars.

The general history of the Hospitalars does not form a portion of my subject, and is also, I presume, more or less known to the greater part of my readers. It is to the peculiarities of their government that I desire to draw attention.

The most important of these consisted in the fact that their Houses, which were erected upon the majority of their estates, were not independent communities, but the officers were in all cases simply stewards of the Prior of England, who in his turn had to account to the head of the Order. Each of these communities, generally consisting of but few members, of whom the majority were usually laymen, with one or more chaplains for the celebration of Divine Offices, was under the government of a Commander or Preceptor, and was hence styled a Commandry or Preceptory. The brethren were allowed a maintenance from the produce of the estates committed to their superintendence, and accounted for the overplus to the Prior at Clerkenwell. Lands, therefore, could only be given to the Order through the Prior, and not to any single Commandry, that being deemed in law incapable of receiving them, as the officers were but "obedientiarii," officials, deputed by the Prior as his representatives and receivers. Their system was, accordingly, entirely different from those of other Orders, that of the Temple excepted. Instead of each being independent, and having the care of its own individual interest, all were so many subject brotherhoods, each acknowledging one general head, and contributing its portion to the general treasury.

This will be sufficient to give the reader a notion of the early history of the Order and its mode of government. We will now proceed to our immediate subject. Let me, however, premise that considerable errors have arisen from the identity of its name with that of numerous other localities possessed of a similar cognomen. This has, unhappily, tended to confuse and falsify, and so to render worse than useless, even the few and very meagre notices of it which have hitherto been committed to the press. There is hardly one of the previous writers who has not mistaken it more or less for the Abbey of Buckland in the County of Devon. One has identified it with Buckland S. Mary in Somersetshire. And, strange to add, even the learned Sir Henry Chauncy, in his History of Hertfordshire, has described an imaginary Buckland Monastery in that county, and has given in connection with it some of the earlier facts in the history of our House. It has not been hitherto, however, nor is it now my desire, to dwell upon other men's omissions or mistakes. A much more agreeable and valuable task is mine, to which I contentedly and gladly turn.

It was about the year 1166, that William de Erlegh, lord of the manor of Durston, founded the House for a small community of Augustine Canons. His father, John de Erlegh, who died in the previous year, was possessed of several manors in the county of Somerset, one of which still bears his name in Somerton Erle, and is mentioned as paying five marcs for scutage in 1161. In behalf of the souls of King Henry and of Alianor the Queen, and of King Henry his son and their other sons and daughters, and for the benefit of the souls of himself and of his wife, this William de Erlegh gave, as Brother John Stillingflete informs us, all the land of Buklande, and the Church of Perretone (Petherton),* with other churches and lands in divers places, as appears by a charter for that purpose made, for the planting and ordaining of Religion at Buckland, by the hand of his kinsman S. Thomas of Canterbury; and that the said Canons thus planted and ordained should possess the aforesaid lands and churches to their proper uses in pure and perpetual alms.†

According to the same chronicler, who wrote an account of the Order in 1434, for a perpetual memorial and commemoration of the various benefactors and their

---

* "The Brooke is caullid Peder, and risith West Sowth West yn the Hylles about a 2 myles of. First it oummith by North-Pedreton, a praty uplandisch Toun, wher is a fair Chirch, the Personage wherof was impropriate to Mynchinbocland."—Leland, Itin. vol. II., p. 66.

† MS. in Off. Armor. L. 17, fol. 153.   MS. Cott. Tib. E. IX., f. 23.
Appendix, No. I.

As will be observed by the references, I am acquainted with two MSS. of this work of Brother John Stillingflete, one preserved in the College of Arms, L. 17., and the other in the Cottonian Library, Tiberius, E. IX. Both are transcripts later by upwards of a century and a half than the lifetime of the chronicler. The former has been much injured by the fire of 1731, and exists but in fragments: the latter is considerably more ample in details, although both of them were evidently copied from a common original, but its text is most corrupt, and the writer was clearly ignorant of the language of the production which he endeavoured to perpetuate.

numerous donations, it appears that together with the Church of Pereton (Petherton), and all its dependent chapels and their appurtenances, the same William de Erlegh gave the Church of Chedsey (Chedzoy), with all the right which the Hospital had or ought to have in the Church of Poulet, with the Chapel of Huntworth, the Chapel of Earl's Neweton, the Chapel of Thurlakeston (although this assuredly was either then or very shortly afterwards appropriated to the Priory of Taunton), the Chapel of Sirdeston, and the Chapel of King's Neweton; also the Church of Bekynton, the Church of Kynmersdon, and the Church of Sirston, with, it is added, other lands and benefactions besides.*

It appears that Walter was the first and possibly the only Prior of the House. The chronicler just quoted is silent on the fact, and indeed the whole account is not a little obscure. But, on turning to other MS. sources for information, I find a Walter Prior of Bokeland, or Bokland, as witness in two documents belonging to this period. One of these sets forth that Alan de Furvell, or Fervell, gave to the Church of S. Andrew of Wells the Church of Cudeworth with the Chapel of Cnolle, to be a perpetual prebend of that Church.† The other is a confirmation by Maude Chandos of a donation of Silvanus to the Church of S. Mary of Stowey, at its dedication, of two acres of land, and of a later donation to the same Church of an acre and a half in Betescumbe; and also of a donation of Roger de Paris to the same Church at the aforesaid dedication of an acre of land in Bucli.‡ Probably, as he is not mentioned in connection with the subsequent troubles, he

* MS. in Off. Armor. L. 17, fol. 153b. Appendix, No. II.
† MS. Harl. 6968, p. 40. Reg. Well., f. 38.
‡ MS. Harl. 6968, Cart. p. 21.

died before the arrival of the evil days which made his House notorious. Indeed, it is not improbable that those troubles were associated with the election of his successor.

A few years after their foundation, these Canons were removed from their monastery. The exact circumstances are nowhere recorded, but it appears that a violent altercation had unhappily arisen which resulted in the death of their steward, who was a relative of the pious founder. A sentence of outlawry was accordingly passed upon them, their House was declared to be forfeited, and their lands and churches were made over by the then sovereign, King Henry the Second,* with the concurrence of Ralph Archbishop of Canterbury, of Reginald Bishop of Bath, and of many of the chief men of England both clerical and lay, to Garner of Naples, Prior of the Hospital of S. John of Jerusalem in England. Among the earliest records of this transfer, for the original deed has not to my knowledge been preserved, is a charter of "inspeximus" granted by K. John, recounting at large the possessions of the Hospitalars, and concluding with the usual forms of confirmation of all previous donations, together with express mention of the arrangement to be noticed immediately. This charter was dated at Rouen, 30th of August, 1st of John, A.D. 1199.†

As I have already hinted, it was not a simple transfer, but a very important stipulation was introduced into the grant, and directed to be fully and faithfully observed. It appears that there were a few Sisters belonging to the Order, who resided at several of the Commandries, as at Hamton near Kyngeston, Kerebrooke, Swynfeld, and other places. It was now ordered and agreed to that these

---

* MS. in Coll. Arm., L. 17, f. 155. Appendix, No. III.
† Rot. Cart. 1 John, m. 17.

ladies should be removed from their various places of residence and be placed in one common and conventual home at Buckland, and that the Order should have no Sisterhood belonging to it in England save and except in this House alone. This occurred about the year 1180, or sometime about fifteen years after the original foundation.

The displaced Canons were removed by Garner, with the King's consent, to certain monasteries, selected probably for their high character and the sound state of their internal discipline. Three were, on their own petition, consigned to the Hospital at Clerkenwell, and assumed the habit of the Order; two were placed by Reginald Bishop of Bath, also on their own petition, in the Priory of Taunton; one in the Priory of Berlitz, and one in that of S. Bartholomew, in Smithfield. These preliminary arrangements being satisfactorily concluded, the main design was forthwith carried out. The Sisters hitherto residing, as already stated, in several of the preceptories, were brought together and lodged at what was henceforth called Mynchin or Nuns' Buckland. From the names which have been preserved, they appear to have been at least nine in number:—Sister Milisent, previously living at Standon, in Hertfordshire; Sister Johanna, at Hamton, in Middlesex; Sister Basilia, at Kerebrooke, in Norfolk; Sister Amabilia and Sister Amicia, of Malketon, at Shenegey, in Cambridgeshire; Sister Christina, of Hoggeshawe, at Hoggeshawe, in Buckinghamshire; Sister Petronilla, at Gosford, in Oxfordshire; and Sister Agnes, at Clanefelde, also in Oxfordshire. They were located at Buckland, that, as it was solemnly added, they and their successors might serve God in that place for ever.* Such was the small beginning, and such the first members of this afterwards famous Sisterhood.

* MS. in Coll. Arm., L. 17, fol. 153. Appendix, No. IV.

From a very interesting list of some of the immediate successors of Prior Garner, contained in one of the Cottonian MSS., specially intended, as it would appear, to illustrate the history of Buckland, we learn that the first Prioress was named Fina. This lady, who died about the year 1240, governed the House for the long space of sixty years, and outlived from the date of her appointment seven successive Heads of the Order.* She was greatly revered, and, as we shall notice subsequently, was specially remembered in the prayers of the Sisterhood for a considerable period after her decease.

The maintenance of these religious women was provided for by a series of benefactors. First on the list is Matilda Countess of Clare, wife of William Earl of Clare, and mother of Richard Earl of Clare, who gave to the Hospital the advowson of the Church of S. Peter of Kerebrooke, and the Preceptory of that name. She gave also to the Sisters of Buckland a pension of 13s. 4d., to be paid by the Preceptor for the time being, and many other benefactions. The gift is recorded to have been made at Westminster, in the fifth year of King Richard I, 1193, in the time of Alan, Prior of England and subsequently Bishop of Bangor.† That of Kerebrooke, however, at least, must be placed at an earlier date, as we have already seen that the Order was in possession of it in the year 1180.

Gilbert de Veer, Prior of the Hospital of S. John of Jerusalem, gave the Sisters an annual pension of one hundred shillings, issuing from the manor of Reynham.‡ He died 13th August, 1198 (?).

---

* MS. Cott. Nero, E. vi. f. 457b. Appendix, No. V.
† MS. in Coll. Arm. L. 17. fol. 148 b. Appendix, No. VI.
‡ MS. Cott. Nero. E. IV. f. 467b. Appendix, No. VII.

Hugh Wallis, Bishop of Lincoln, by his will, made in the year 1211, left the sum of twenty marcs "ad fabricam ecclesiæ de Bokland." This structure, it appears, was dedicated to the Blessed Virgin and S. Nicholas.*

Hugh de Alneto, or D'Auncy, Prior of the Hospital of S. John of Jerusalem, gave, with the consent of the Chapter, permission to the Lady Loretta, Countess of Leicester, to find a Chaplain to celebrate daily the mass of the Virgin in the Church of the Sisters, in return for certain lands and rents which the Countess gave to the Hospital, to be converted to the proper uses of the Sisters aforesaid of Buckland, so that the aforesaid Chaplain should be deputed to no other service save the proper and peculiar ministry of the Virgin in the Church aforesaid.† We possess the charter of the Countess of Leicester contained in one of "inspeximus" and confirmation granted shortly after by King Henry III., and dated at Westminster, the 16th of July, 1227. As it is of considerable interest, both from its subject matter and from the names of the places with which it furnishes us, some of my readers may be glad to have it in a literal translation. It is as follows :—

"Be it known to all the faithful of Christ, as well present as future, who shall see or hear this writing, that I Loretta, Countess of Leycester, have given and granted to God, and Blessed Mary, and S. John Baptist, and the blessed Poor of the House of the Hospital of Jerusalem, towards the sustenance of the Sisters of Boclaund serving God, and towards the finding of a certain Chaplain in the same House, who daily and for ever may celebrate mass in honor of the Blessed Virgin Mary, in the greater Church

* Rot. Chart. 1 Joh. m. 17.
† MS. Cott. Tib. E. IX. f. 23. MS. in Coll. Arm. L. 17. f. 153 b. Appendix, No. VIII.

at Bokland, at the altar of the Blessed Virgin, for the health of my soul and of Lord Robert my husband, some time Earl of Leicester, and for the health of the souls of my father and mother, and of all my ancestors and successors, all my land of Noteston, and all my land of Ynesford, this side the water and that side the water, and sixty-four acres of my demesne above Ruwedon, and all my land of Ridescot, and of Hele, and of Chorlecot, and of Tunecote, and of Boteburn, and all the land which Philip at Way holds, with the tenants of the aforesaid lands. Moreover, a hundred acres of my demesne in Bremesmore, and my wood which is called Anerwd, and one ferling at Roitheye, with all their appurtenances in the manor of Toustoke, with pasturage and all other things appertaining to the aforesaid lands. Moreover, all kinds of common between my tenements wheresoever. To be holden and possessed freely and quietly in perpetual and pure alms, as any alms may be freely and quietly given. And that this my gift may in future times obtain the strength of perpetual firmness, I have held it right to strengthen it by the defence of the present writing with the apposition of my seal. Witnesses, Master Lambert, Sub-dean of Wells; Lord Philip de Alben; Lord Roger de la Zuche; Adam, son of Hondebrand; Master Humphrey, Canon of Cycester; Master Reginald de Merestone; William, Chaplain of Bukingeham; Walter, clerk of Langeham; Thomas, clerk of Glouecester; Nicholas de Wyleye, and others." *

Other early gifts, of which the exact dates have not been preserved, are the following :—

Ralph, the son of William de Briwere, gave to the Sisters the Church of Tolland with its appurtenances.

---

* Cart. 11 Hen. III., p. 2, m. 9. Appendix, No. IX.

Alan, son of Antony Russell, gave them the Church of Donington, in the diocese of Lincoln.

Warin de Aula gave them Bodescombe.

Ascuid Musard gave them Chiltcombe, Wysangre, and Bochelcote.

And Robert Arundale gave them Halse, with its appurtenances.* Probably this gift is the same as that subsequently mentioned, as having been made so late as the year 1374, and as the subject of legal investigation in the year 1400. The name, however, of the donor is there given as Roger Arundell.

Muriel de Bohun gave them 40 solidatæ of land in Sherborn and Prumesley, in the county of Dorset, which grant was confirmed by her husband, Ralph de Bruere.†

The Prioress of Buckland held also one fee in Primesleigh, which was Robert de London's, of the Bishop of Salisbury; and, with William Waddam, half a fee, which was Robert de London's, of the same Bishop in chief.‡

By a charter dated at Henbiry, the 3rd of August, 1228, King Henry III. granted the Sisters permission to take from his park of Neuton a cartload of dead wood for fuel every week in the year. And it was considerately added, that, because it was more convenient to remove the aforesaid firewood in summer than in winter, the king permitted them to take the stated number of cartloads in the interval from Easter to the feast of S. Peter ad vincula, the 1st of August. An order was given to Richard de Wrotham, to allow them to remove the fuel, in agreement with the terms of the king's grant. ||

* MS. Cott. Tib. E. IX. f. 23. MS. in Off. Armor. L. 17. f. 153 b. Appendix, No. X.
† *Hutchins's Dorsetshire*, II., p. 394.   ‡ *Ib.*
|| Pat. 12 Henry III., m. 2. Appendix, No. XI.

It would appear that this privilege was not only one of considerable value, as it would necessarily be, but also one which was subject to frequent invasion, for we find a long series of confirmations of this and similar grants. In some instances it was possibly the change of the officer to whom the park was intrusted, which necessitated the preparation of a new instrument. On the 3rd of April, 1229, the king signified from Marlborough to Hugh de Nevill his royal pleasure that the Sisters should have weekly from his park of Neuton one cartload of the dead wood of that park for their fuel. A similar permission was added to remove the whole of their yearly gathering between the feast of Easter and that of S. Peter ad vincula, instead of employing the winter in so inconvenient a work.* A similar order was given to Richard de Wrotham, dated at Westminster, 15th of May, 1229.†

Immediately subsequent to this grant, a very interesting addition was made to the revenues of the Sisters, and again it was by their royal benefactor. The letters were addressed to the King's treasurer and chamberlains. "Know ye," he says, "that we have given, and granted, and by our charter have confirmed to the Prioress of Bocland and the Sisters there serving God, of the Order of the Hospital of Jerusalem, to maintain three maidens for ever in the said priory, a delivery of two pence and one half-penny, which Roger, Chaplain of the Bishop of Lincoln, used to receive daily by the hand of the Sheriff of Hereford our almoner; and a delivery of two pence, which Margary, the nurse of Isabella our sister, used to receive daily by the hand of the same. To be held of us and of our heirs by them and their successors in free, pure, and perpetual alms; and to

* Claus. 13 Hen. III., m. 12.
† Claus. 13 Hen. III., m. 10.

be received for ever at our exchequer; that is to say, one half at Michaelmas, and the other at Easter. And so we command you that ye have these deliveries made unto them, as aforesaid. At Faversham, the 20th of September, 1229."*

This was followed eight days afterwards by a grant, addressed to Richard de Wrotham, in favour of the Sisters, increasing the gift of one to that of three weekly cartloads of wood for their fire. It was to be taken every week "de spinis, alno, et arabili," in the park of Neuton, and a similar concession was added as to time with that previously stated. The grant was dated at Westminster, 28th September, 1229.† A similar one was addressed two days afterwards to John de Monem, from London, the 30th of September, 1229.‡

Terric de Nussa, Prior of England, who died on the 21st December, 1237, gave the Sisters and their successors, by advice of the general Chapter of his brethren, an annual allowance of thirty-eight marcs, twelve shillings, and eight pence sterling, which they were to receive from the Preceptor of Buckland for the time being, at two terms of the year; namely, at the feast of Easter, nineteen marcs, six shillings and four pence, and a similar sum at the feast of S. Michael. And it was further ordered that the Preceptor or Master should be allowed this amount in his responsions or annual returns to the Receiver General of the Order.‖

Previous to the 15th of February, 1270-1, which was the day of his decease, Roger de Veer, Prior of England, paid a

---

* Pat. 13 Hen. III., m. 4.
† Claus. 13 Hen. III., m. 4.
‡ Claus. 13 Hen. III., m. 3.
‖ MS. in Coll. Arm., L. 17, f. 153. Appendix, No. XII.

visit to Bukland to inspect the state of the House. He found great difference and discord prevailing between the Preceptor and the Prioress and Convent, about a number of matters intimately affecting the Prioress and her Sisters. There is little doubt, as in an instance which will be before us presently, that the Preceptor looked with a grudging eye on the possessions of the Sisterhood, and hardly endured to part with the funds which he was compelled to advance for their maintenance. Roger appears to have felt that nothing but peremptory measures would ensure peace. With the assent of his chapter at Melcheburn, he made among other regulations the following :—That the Prioress and Convent should have their own steward, who should sit at the table of the Preceptor; and one servant, who should sit with the servants of the Preceptor ; and who should be there daily at table unless the steward should otherwise appoint him. That at the feast of S. Michael, when the steward should desire to hold his court at Hele, he should have of the cellarer five white loaves and his flagons full of ale ; and that at the same feast, when he should hold his courts at Kinmersdon and Primmilegh, he should have the same ; and at Hokeday the same; and that he should have his horse furniture and all other necessaries, at the delivery and appointment of the Prioress and Convent. And that, if in anything he should be at fault, it should be lawful for the Prioress to prohibit him from meddling with their goods, but not to remove him from his office without the consent of the Prior. Moreover, it was ordained that the Sisters should have a secular priest to celebrate mass for the soul of Sister Fina sometime Prioress there, and for the souls of the founders and benefactors of the said House, who should sit at table with the brethren, and have his bed in the dormitory between the priests and clerks, and for the rest of his time should be at the order of the Prioress; so that the Preceptor should have an allowance of five marcs for the table of the said priest, and also of the one brother who celebrated the mass of Blessed Mary, and also three shillings at the feast of S. Michael for the clerk of the chapel.* The calm which this arrangement produced was at best but temporary, and we shall soon have to notice some evidences of the feeling with which it was regarded by the Preceptor and his brethren, by whom the establishment of the neighbouring Community was clearly considered a grievance of no common order!

In or about the year 1270, the Hospitallers of Boclande were returned among other Somersetshire landowners as holding five virgates of land, of the annual value of fifty shillings.†

In 1276, the Sisters are stated on the verdict of a jury to have common of pasture for eight oxen and two cows in a place of forty acres situated in Rolneston.‡

Shortly after this date the chapel of Kynmeresdon was sacrilegiously broken into and plundered. The crime was charged upon a certain Robert de Bo——, (the MS. is imperfect and the name cannot be regained) before the Justices Itinerant, but he was happy enough to clear himself to the satisfaction of his judges. A letter is extant from Robert Bishop of Bath to the King, "excellentissimo domino suo domino Edwardo," wishing him health "in Eo per Quem reges regnant et regnorum omnium gubernacula sustentantur," and soliciting the prompt restoration of the possessions and goods of the accused, which had been

---

* MS. in Off. Arm. L. 17, f. 153 b. Appendix, No. XIII.
† Test. de Nevill, f. 759.
‡ Hilar. an. 4 Edw. I. de Jur. et Ass. rot. 14. Abbrev. Plac. p. 189.

detained during the process of the investigation. The Bishop's letter is dated at Windsor, 9th September, 1281.*

In 1290 was the famous Taxatio of Pope Nicholas IV. The Church of Boclonde was then valued at £5 6s. 8d; Perton, with its Chapel, at £53 6s. 8d.; the Vicarage of the same at £6 13s. 4d.; and Elleworth, at £4 6s. 8d.†

The favour of collecting fire wood from the park of Neuton, Perton, or Petherton, appears, as I have remarked, to have been often contested. In the year 1290, the nuns were obliged to petition the king in parliament with a view to the restoration of their rights. They submitted that since the battle of Evesham, A.D. 1265, they had been hindered in their ancient privilege, and humbly solicited the king's favour in the restitution of the same.‡

Richard de Plessetis, or de Placey, a descendant of Richard de Wrotham already noticed, who died 20 Edw. I., 1292, founded, about two years before his decease, a perpetual chantry at Newton for the health of his soul and the souls of his father and mother, and all his ancestors and successors. For the endowment of the same, he granted to William de Hilprinton, the intended chantry priest, and his successors, in the chapel of S. Peter at Newton, a house in which William de Grey, a former chaplain, lived aforetime, and several acres of land in Ivymore, Highmore, and Ellerhaye, together with the tithes of Newton and Petherton Park, and right of common for six oxen and six heifers in all places where he had common. The witnesses to this charter were the Preceptor of Buckland, Sir Geoffrey de Wrockshall, Sir John de Placetis, Peter de Hamme, and John de Marisco.‖

* Calendar of Letters, No. 1949.
† Tax. Eccl. P. Nich. IV., pp. 198, 199.
‡ Pet. in Parl., 18 Edw. I., n. 152, vol. I., 58.
‖ Collins. e Regist. Well. III. 65.

In 1297, the 25th of Edward I., the Master of the Hospital of Bocland was returned from the counties of Somerset and Dorset, as holding lands or rents to the amount of £20 yearly value or upwards, either *in capite* or otherwise, and as such he was summoned under the general writ to perform military service, &c., in parts beyond the sea. The muster was at London, on the Sunday next after the Octave of S. John the Baptist, or the 7th of July, 1297.*

In the Perambulation of the Forest of North Petherton, dated the 25th of May, 26 Edward I., 1298, it is set forth that John de Erlegh holds the manor of North Petherton, with the moors, &c., and that the Prior of S. John of Jerusalem holds the hamlet of Gogestode, the Priory of Bokeland, the hamlets of Taklestone and Heggynge, with the woods, moors, marshes, &c., and the hamlet of Bidone, with the moors, marshes, &c.†

King Edward I. gave the Order a charter for a weekly market, held on Monday, in his manor of Halse.‡

The year 1306 brought a further increase of property. A writ was addressed on the 16th of October, 1305, and an inquest was held at Somerton, before J. de Montacute, the King's Escheator, on the Monday after Palm Sunday in the following year, or the 28th of March, 1306, to examine and report whether it were to the detriment of the King, or of any others, if Thomas de Berkelay should give two shops, with their appurtenances, in Welles, to the Prioress and Sisters of Boclande. The process was exactly similar to that which I have fully explained in my History of Taunton Priory, and does not require further illustration.

* Parl. Writs, I., 293.
† Per. For. de North Petherton, 26 Edward I.
‡ Cart. 18 Edw. I., n. 80. MS. Coll. Arm., L. 17. f. 156. Appendix, No. XIV.

The verdict was favourable, and the King's letters patent, dated at Lanercost, the 20th of October, enabled both parties to act in agreement with the donor's desire.* The annual value of the property was eighteen shillings in all issues.

William de Tottehale, Prior of England, presented John de Messingham to North Pederton, 12th March, 1309-10.†
The year subsequent to this date, the same Thomas de Berkelee granted under very peculiar circumstances four pounds of rent, with appurtenances, issuing from lands and tenements in Hamme, held by Thomas de Stane of the the said Thomas. This sum was to be received by the Prioress and Sisters in aid of the maintenance of his daughter Isabella, who was a Sister of the House. They were to receive it during the life of this lady; and after her decease it was to revert entirely to its former master. The letters patent describe the Priory as very poor, "quod nimis exile esse dinoscitur," and convey the King's license for this seasonable help. They are dated at London, the 25th of August, 1311.‡

The Master of the Hospital was certified, pursuant to writ tested at Clipston, 5th March, 1316, as one of the lords of the township of North Petherton.‖

In the Ordination of the Vicarage of Poulet, made in the following year, the Vicar was to pay every year one marc of silver to the Sisters of Bokland.§

On the 9th of March, 1320, John de Werewell was Preceptor, and was appointed by the Prior of S. John to

---

* Inquis. ad. 9, d. 34 Edw. I., n. 178. Pat. 34 Edw. I., m. 4.
† MS. Harl. 6985 B, f. 126 b.
‡ Pat. 5 Edw. II., p. 1, m. 20.
‖ Parl. Writs, II., 378.
§ MS. Harl. 6968, Cart. p. 7.

be procurator and administrator of the estates belonging to the Hospital in the diocese of Bath and Wells.*

In the year 1328, an amicable arrangement was after some delay arrived at between Geoffrey Samuel and William his son on the one part, and the Prioress Isabella la Louwe and Convent on the other, touching the celebration of Divine Service in their chapel of Lokyngton, in their parish of Kilmersdon. It was agreed that the Prioress and Convent, for themselves and their successors, should grant to the aforesaid Geoffrey and William, the celebration in the aforesaid chapel, on Sundays, Wednesdays, and Fridays, to be performed by the perpetual Vicar of Kilmersdon, in return for a tenement which the Prioress and Convent held of the fee of the aforesaid Geoffrey and William. To the constant maintenance of this celebration, Geoffrey and William bound themselves and their heirs in one quarter of corn, to be paid every year to the said Vicar from their manor of Lokyngton. The confirmation was dated the 19th of November, 1328.†

On the 28th of August in the following year, 1329, died Thomas L'Archier, Prior of England. He gave to the Sisters of Buckland a yearly pension of forty shillings, to be drawn for ever from the manor of Hidon, a limb of Templecomb.‡

During the same year, the Preceptor and Sisters were obliged to call in the aid of their ecclesiastical superiors against the harsh measures of Master Richard de Thistelden, their diocesan's official. The latter had called upon them to exhibit their title to the churches of Northpederton, Durston, Halse, Bromfeld, and Kynemersden, in the

* Archer, e Reg. Drok. 159.
† MS. Harl, 6964, p. 132.
‡ MS. Cott. E. vi. f. 467b. Appendix, No. XV.

diocese of Bath and Wells. These churches were, as we have already noticed, canonically appropriated to them, and had been so from ancient times. On their citation to pay the customary "obedience" in behalf of these churches, considerable harshness was exhibited; and, on their duly demanding to be furnished with a copy of his commission, the commissary had not only neither listened to their prayer nor acceded to their request, but had pronounced them contumacious, when they were not so, had fined them in an immoderate sum of money, and had ordered the same to be levied forthwith. An appeal was forwarded to the Apostolic See, which was promptly followed by an inhibition against his attempting aught to the prejudice of the appellants during the pending of the suit in the Court of Canterbury. The inhibition was dated at London, the 26th of September, 1329.*

It appears, from the Year Book of 1330, that the arrangement just mentioned in connexion with the chapel of Lokyngton, or Leeke, was not fully and faithfully observed. The record referred to presents us, accordingly, with an instance of litigation, the issue of which, so far as we can gather it, was of an unfavourable character. The proceedings, as there given, are in avowry, and the question is raised as to the lawfulness of a certain distress levied by Agnes, widow of William Samuel, upon Isabel de Berch, Prioress of Buckland, through the alleged non-performance of the terms of the covenant. Agnes, by a plaint sued by the Prioress, is made defendant, and called upon to give reasons for levying the distress. To those of my readers who feel an interest in the old practice of the law, it will not be unwelcome if I enter into the particulars

* MS. Harl. 6065, p. 17. Appendix, No. XVI.

of the case, and exhibit the process by which an attempt was made to obtain restitution. It is stated that "Agnes Samuel avoweth a distress upon Isabel de Berch, Prioress of Buckland, by reason that one M., a predecessor of the said Isabel, held of Richard Flory a message and acre of land by fealty and the service of finding a chaplain to sing, in the chapel within his manor of Leeke, masses, matins, and vespers, on three days in the week throughout the whole year, to wit Sunday, Wednesday, and Friday, and to find in the same chapel bread, and wine, and other things suitable for the celebration of Divine Service, "pan', et vine, et auters ornam'ts pur divines servic' celebrer," of which services Richard was seised; the which Richard gave and granted the manor, with the chapel to which the services related, to William the late husband of the same Agnes, and to Agnes, and to the heirs of their two bodies; the which M. made attornment of the said services to William and Agnes; and after the death of William this same Agnes was seised, by the hand of the said Isabel, &c., and for the singing in arrear for two years.*

The defence that seems by the pleadings to have been set up to Agnes Samuel's case was that the Vicar by a certain composition received a quarter of wheat for the fulfilment of the duties, which were performed by a priest employed by him. And the question was whether the facts alleged by the Prioress were sufficient answer to bar Agnes Samuel of her action, or whether on the other hand she were justified in levying the distress. We do not know the issue, as, the Court sitting in Banco and not at Nisi prius, no decision was come to on the

* Mich. 4 Edw. III., pl. 52.

merits; though I think, as I have already said, that it may be gathered from the pleadings that Prioress would be unsuccessful, and that the distress which Agnes Samuel had levied would be pronounced valid and according to law.

Of the year 1335 I am happy to furnish a very valuable memorial. It is the certificate of the Lord Bishop to the King, of the churches, advowsons, and pensions which the Prior and Brethren of the Hospital possessed in the diocese of Bath and Wells. They are here stated to hold, as appropriate rectories, the Church of Halse, of the annual value of £10; the Church of Durston, with the tithes of Coggelode by Boelande, (there is still a "Coglett Field" in the immediate neighbourhood of the site of the Priory) of the annual value of 8 marcs; the Church of Northpederton, of the annual value of 60 marcs; and the Church of Kynemersdone, of the annual value of 24 marcs. They have also, it is added, the advowsons of the Churches of Ellesworthe, taxed in 6 marcs and a half; of Talande, taxed in 3 marcs; and of Hethfeld, taxed in 5 marcs. They have also the following annual pensions: from the Chapel of Bodyngton in the park of Netherstauway, 2s.; from the Church of Touland, 2s.; from Bekyngton, 20s.; and from the Church of Poulet, 1 marc. The document is dated at Banwell, 27th August, 1335.*

In the 11th year of King Edward III., 1337, died John de Erlegh, seised at the time of his decease of the manors of Durston, North Petherton, Somerton Erle, Bekington, Michaelchurch, &c. The fact of special interest in our present enquiry is that he left behind him a son John, born

* MS. Harl. 6965, p. 93.

and baptised at Durston, 29th of November, 6 Edward
III., 1332, who afterwards attended the Black Prince to
Spain; another son Richard; and three daughters, Katharine Prioress of Buckland, Elizabeth wife of Sir John
Stafford, and Alice wife of Sir Nicholas Poines.* Here
we have an instance, by no means uncommon, of a noble
daughter of the house of a founder governing the Community which owed its origin to the piety of an ancestor
long gone to his reward.

For the year subsequent to this date we possess an
invaluable series of returns, which furnish us with a most
lively picture of the system of the Hospital in full operation
and activity. It will be remembered that, in the sketch
which I gave of the Order, I showed that all the provincial
Heads and Preceptors were simply delegates of the Prior of
England, and had to account to him for the surplus of their
receipts over their expenditure. The Hospital in England
was only a portion of that widely-spread institution which
had possessions in at least two-thirds of the then known
world. An annual return was accordingly made from each
of the Preceptories or Commandries by the Preceptor or
receiver to the Prior of England, and by him to the headquarters of the Order, wherever those might happen to be.
Happily for us, we possess one of these interesting balance-sheets, that for the year 1338, which was fortunately
discovered at Malta, and published three years ago by the
Camden Society, with an admirable preface by my lamented
friend, Mr. John Mitchell Kemble. This truly valuable
contribution to historical and archæological science would,
in my humble opinion, be perfect, but for the grave mistake,
for which my friend was not responsible, of printing the

* Inq. p. m. 28 Edw. III., n. 71.

MS. *in extenso*, the result of which is that certain errors run through the whole volume, a result but poorly compensated for by the imagined—and only imagined—greater facility with which the accounts may be perused. To well-instructed antiquaries it is as easy to read manuscripts with their contractions as *in extenso*, while to general readers the matter presented in either form is equally obscure and unintelligible.

The return itself consists of a minutely-accurate balance-sheet for every part of the property of the Order in England, with an exact account of income and of outlay in every *bajulia*, bailiwick or manor. Buckland figures prominently among these; and I will endeavour, by means of the data here presented to us, to give my reader a picture of the scene on which we are now engaged, as it appeared during the former half of the fourteenth century.

The establishment consisted of various buildings, of which three are mentioned, which either required some outlay, or furnished a source of income. First, there was the court or manor-house, but it sadly needed a new roof. The bakehouse attached to it also wanted repair, and is described as in a very ruinous condition. A dovecot, which, singularly enough, appears to have been an appendage to almost every House, and a never-failing source of emolument, is returned as yielding, together with the produce and herbage of the garden, the considerable annual value of 10s. The proceeds of both were no doubt disposed of in the neighbourhood, when the supply exceeded the need at home. As that supply would necessarily vary with different years, it is not unlikely, especially as we constantly find this item set down in round numbers throughout the various accounts, that it was computed at a certain annual value, which in some years was exceeded by the actual return, while in others it was deficient. Attached to the Community was a demesne of 268 acres of arable land, of which 200 were valued at 12d. an acre ; and the remaining 68 at 7d. an acre, amounting together to £12 16s. There were also 42 acres of meadow, whereof three were taken by the Sisters. Of the remaining 39 the value of each was 2s., and of the whole 78s. There was also a small church, "una parva ecclesia," appropriated to the Priory, of the annual value of 40s. Two mills were an additional source of income, which, with assessed rent, paid by free tenants to their landlord, amounted to £10. The fines and perquisites of the manor courts were valued at 20s. The *confraria*, or voluntary contribution from the neighbourhood, whether constant or exceptional is uncertain, hardly produced this year the sum of 80 marcs.

Halse is returned as a "member" of this bailiwick. It also had a manor house, but in a state of still greater dilapidation than that of Buckland. "Destructa" it was, "et multum vastata;" so much so that the proceeds of the manor for a whole year would scarce be sufficient to repair the damage. 220 acres were attached to it, 200 of which were valued at 12d., and 20 at 10d. an acre, together £10 16s. 8d. There were 28 acres of pasture, valued at 8d. an acre ; 18 acres and a half of meadow, valued at 2s. an acre; 52 acres of pasture, valued at 4d. an acre; assessed rent £20 3s. per annum ; fines and perquisites of the manor courts, 40s. ; works and customary services of the native villani, commuted, I presume, into a money-rent, 40s.; the appropriated rectory, valued at 18 marcs ; and pasture in moor and wood, at 6s. 8d.

The total amount of receipt and profit from the entire manor, with its member, was 186 marcs, 10s. 4d.

We will now turn to the other side of the account, and

here we shall have an interesting and necessarily faithful picture of the social life of the House.

The Society consisted, in the first place, of the Preceptor and five Brethren, after whom were their servants of various kinds, and the stranger guests, whom their rule of hospitality obliged them to entertain. The cost of 94 quarters of wheat, which were made into bread for the House, at 3s. a quarter, amounted to £14 2s. For their beer, 130 quarters of grain, of which 52 were of barley, at 2s. a quarter, and 78 of oat malt, at 20d. a quarter, both amounting to £11 14s. Then there were the expenses of the kitchen, an outlay of 4s. a-week, or £10 8s. a year. The robes, mantles, and other necessaries of the Preceptor and his five Brethren, are stated at £10 8s., allowing £1 14s. 3d. to each, which, as it appears throughout the returns, was the stated and ordinary sum. The stipend of a chaplain, per annum, with a seat at the Preceptor's table, 20s. John le Port, a corrodary, or fellow-commoner, by deed of the chapter, had a seat at the table, valued at 18s. In the robes of the Preceptor's servants was expended 1 marc. In the stipends of four clerks of the confraria, with commons, £4. In the wages of various servants, the cook, baker, steward, porter, woodreeve, chapel-clerk, gardener, swineherd, and carter, 51s. 8d., of whom four received 2 marcs, and each of the rest 5s. The stipends of four pages amounted to 8s. They spent during the year, in repairs and roofing of their buildings, 40s. The visitation of the Prior of England, whose duty it was to make in person his annual examination, cost during the six days of his presence the heavy sum of £6. Lastly there was the annual pension to the Sisters, which we have already noticed, amounting to the charge of 29 marcs. The sum total of all the expenses and payments is 125 marcs, 3s. And the surplus, to be paid to the general treasury of the Order, figures at 61 marcs, 7s. 4d.

The Preceptor and his brethren who at this time represented the Hospital at Buckland were Brother John Diluwe, Preceptor, chaplain; Brother Robert Mountfort, chaplain ; Brother Adam de Catworth, chaplain ; Brother Thomas de Taimeworth, chaplain; Brother Andrew de Shafteworth, sergeant-at-arms ; and Brother Henry de Whaddon, sergeant-at-arms and steward of the Sisters. To these we must add John le Port, the corrodary, to whom we have already referred.

The return concludes with an account of the Sisterhood. It describes their House as having been founded by the kings of England, and themselves as wearing the habit of the Hospital, and as commonly amounting to fifty in number. It further states that, by the ordination of their founders, their possessions were managed by themselves. Intent on making a correct report, and with a scarcely disguised feeling of resentment against everything which could tend to diminish the surplus by which his activity and good management could best be exhibited, the Preceptor most ungallantly adds that he and his brethren neither did nor could have or get aught from these ladies, "sed potius onus et gravamen," but rather burden, charge, and grievance— inasmuch as by a fixed ordination they were to have a brother of the Priory of England, at the expense of the Prior and Preceptor of the place, to be their steward, and two brethren for chaplains, and one secular chaplain to serve their church—also, it is not omitted to add, at the expense of the Preceptor. In the same place they had three carucates of land, of the annual value, in common years, of £6. Besides this, they are described as being in possession of other property, with some of which we are already acquainted:—at Thele, in Devonshire, one carucate of land, of the value of 40s.; at Prunslee, one carucate, valued at 40s.; at Kynemersdon, one carucate, valued at 50s. Of assessed rent, they are stated to own 90 marcs, but it is added that hardly so many as 80 are levied. The following churches also are mentioned as appropriated to them:—The church of Pederton, of the value of 50 marcs; the church of Kynemersdon, of the value of 20 marcs; and that of Bromfeld, valued at £10. All of which, is the conclusion forcibly impressed upon the treasurer, are insufficient to provide for the maintenance of the Sisters and that of their servants, together with the repairs of their buildings, their dress, and other necessaries, apart from the help of friends and elemosynary payments.* It is indeed clear that a Community of fifty nuns, with their servants, although they did not afterwards, or perhaps often, amount to half so many, would be very inadequately maintained out of the funds thus described as being at their disposal, and that they would require the assistance of powerful patrons to enable them to support a bare existence.

From Hidon, a limb of Temple Combe, the same record informs us that they had 3 marcs per annum for a tenement of theirs there.† This, as we have already noticed, was given them by Prior Thomas L'Archer, who died in 1329.

I may here place on record that William Redmor was presented to the Church of Hethfeld by Philip de Thame, Prior of England, on the 4th of February, 1348.‡ It would appear that he did not long retain his benefice; for John de Donne, Rector of the Church of Hethfeld,

---

* Hosp. in Engl. pp. 17—20.
† Hosp., p. 205.
‡ MS. Harl. 6965, p. 201.

presented Robert atte Crosse, Priest, to the Church of Fydyngton on the 25th of June, 1354. The institution is dated at Wylescomb, the 17th of the following month.*

The pension of 20s. due from the Church of Bekyngton had to be recovered by law in 1353. A writ was addressed for this purpose to John de Werdyr, the parson, on the 12th of July in that year.†

In connexion with Buckland, it will not be amiss to repeat that Roger Arundell, sometime lord of the manor of Halse, gave that manor, in the year 1374, to the Prior of S. John of Jerusalem in England, on condition that he and his successors should find and maintain a chapel at Halse, and a chaplain to celebrate Divine Service for ever in the same for the souls of Roger, his predecessors, and all the faithful departed. A jury found the facts aforesaid, and that the manor, which was held of the king in capite, as of his manor of Hampstede Mareschall, by military service, was of the annual value in all issues of £20. The same jury found that Roger Torell had given to the Rector of the Church of Mulverton 20 acres of arable land, called Mynsterlond in Mulverton, to find a chaplain who should celebrate Divine Service three days every week in the chapel of Torelles Preston. The land was held of the king in capite, by military service, and was worth in all issues 16s. per annum. The Jurors were Bartholomew Baghey, Adam Londe, Robert Ladell, Walter Cherl, Richard Hokeday, John Holm, Benedict Flamesy, Robert Hewere, John Garland, Thomas Clyve, Gilbert Stenes, and Robert Skilgate; and the inquest was taken at Taunton, before Adam atte More, the king's escheator, on Wednesday, the 8th of March, 1374. A writ of

* Hyll Cartulary, pp. 52, 53.
† MS. Harl. 6965, p. 257.

"certiorari" in respect of these gifts was issued on the 3rd of July, 1400.*

We must now pass to the year 1387. At this time the Prioress and Sisters obtained from King Richard II., by a fine of thirteen shillings and four pence, another charter of "inspeximus" and confirmation of their ancient grant from Henry III., of fuel from the park of Perton. The letters patent were dated at Westminster, 25th June, 1387.†

At an Inquisition taken at Yvelchester, 7th October, 1398, Roger Mortimer, Earl of March, who died on the previous feast of S. Margaret, July 20, is stated to have been seised at the time of his death of two fees payable by the Prior of S. John, as of the honor of Wiggemor. This is stated in immediate connexion with various other properties of the said Roger at Mershewood, Bocland, and Chilton.‡

On the 28th of April, 1405, another charter of "inspeximus" and ratification was granted to the Prioress and Sisters, on the payment of one marc, in behalf of their ancient privilege. The letters patent on this occasion are particularly valuable, inasmuch as they furnish us with the name of the Prioress of the House, and thus make a still further addition to our list of hitherto unnoted Superiors. The lady in question was named Alicia, but of what family and from whom descended all human record has disappeared. The document is dated at Westminster, on the day and year above mentioned.||

Three years subsequently, on the 14th of November, 1408, a writ of privy seal was issued, which furnishes us

* Inq. ad q.d. 1 Hen. IV., n. 22.
† Pat. 11 Ric. II., p. 1, m. 36.
‡ Inq. p.m. 22 Ric. II., n. 34.
|| Pat. 6 Hen. IV., p. 2, m. 25.

with a considerable amount of information as to the legal position of the Sisters. It is clear, from the very terms of their constitution, that they were necessarily subject to the Prior at Clerkenwell in no inconsiderable degree. Bracton, indeed, specially cites them as instances of legal inability of acting apart from the Prior and Head of their Order.* It appears that the Sisters had represented to the king the ancient grant which had been, as we have seen, conceded to them so early as the reign of Henry III., and the further permission accorded of removing their firewood, for greater convenience, between the Festival of Easter and that of S. Peter ad vincula. It is added, though hardly as it would seem borne out by the facts, that these concessions had been enjoyed by them from that time to the present without let or hindrance either from the king or the custodians of the park. The present keeper, however, had resisted their demand on the ground that they were but officials, "obedienciarie" of the Prior of S. John, and therefore not competent to accept the grant in their own persons. The Prioress and her Sisters, accordingly, petitioned the king to interfere in their behalf and to provide a remedy. This result it is the intention of the writ to effect. The king, taking it into his royal consideration that the Prioress and Sisters would instantly and devoutly pray for the health of himself and his dearest consort Johanna during their lives, and for their souls after their deaths, and for the king's dearest consort Maria, deceased, granted their request, by conveying to Walter Grendon, Prior of S. John, the gift already conceded, so that the same might be to the use and profit of the Prioress and Sisters at Buckland. Various ambiguities also in the

---

* De legibus, lib. v. tr. v. c. 18, de exceptionibus.

original charter were now removed, and the intention of the royal donor made more conspicuous. Perton is changed to Pederton. In the previous instruments they were to take their firewood "de spinis, alno, et arabili:" the grant now ran "videlicet thorn, aller, mapel, et hasell." It was also set forth that each cartload should consist of as much firewood as six horses could draw, and that the servants should fall, cut up and carry away at their will the amount granted to them every year, from the Festival of the Annunciation to the Festival of All Saints, without disturbance, hindrance, or grievance from the king, his heirs, the keeper of the park, or any other official or servant whomsoever.*

King Henry V. confirmed this grant of his father to William Hilles, Prior of S. John, in behalf of the Prioress and Sisters, on the payment of half a marc, at Westminster, on the 8th of February, 1418-9.†

Of this also a confirmation was granted by King Henry VI., at Westminster, on the 5th of February, 1422-3.‡ And another ratification and confirmation of the same, on the payment of half a marc, was made to Robert Botell, Prior of S. John, twenty-one years afterwards, on the 10th of February, 1443-4.‖

The Sisters appear to have struggled against poverty without much aid from those who should seem to have been their natural patrons, but from whom it is clear that they received little sympathy. On the 22nd of April, 1447, they sold their pension of 4 marcs, payable to them

* Pat. 10 Hen. IV., p. 1, m. 19. MS. in Coll. Armor. L. 17, f. 156b. Appendix, No. XVII.
† Pat. 6 Hen. V., m. 10.
‡ Pat. 1 Hen. VI., p. 5, m. 5.
‖ Pat. 22 Hen. VI., p. 2, m. 22.

from the vicarage of North Pederton.* These, it is said by Dr. Archer, are still paid to the Crown.

It would appear, although we know very little either of the process or the results, that several valuations of the property were made during the last half of the fifteenth century, especially in 1460 and 1493. We shall presently have before us, however, a most valuable and complete document of a similar kind, and of so near a period to that of the returns alluded to as to make their absence a matter of less importance.†

For some few years nothing seems to have transpired of which a record is preserved for us; but I have found some documents which belong to the commencement of the following century, which give us an excellent insight into the condition of the House at that period.

I may premise, however, to keep to the chronological order as far as possible, that, at a Chapter holden at Melchborne on the 9th of November, 1500, there was granted to Alexander Verney, Chaplain, a chamber suitable to his rank in the manor of Bodmescomb in the county of Devon, with fuel for the said chamber from the underwood of that manor, eight marcs sterling a year by way of stipend, and for food and raiment, during his life, to be received through the hands of the Preceptor of Buckland, or of the farmer in charge. The said Alexander obliged himself to celebrate Divine Service in the Chapel of Bodmescomb as long as his strength lasted so to do. If, from old age or infirmity, he became unable to officiate, his chamber and allowances were still to be continued to him. If, however, whilst able to celebrate, he failed in his duty, and without

---

* MS. Harl. 6966, p. 61.
† Comput. 38 Hen. VI. Off. Aug. 13092. Comput. 8 Hen. VII. Off. Aug. 1232. Add. MS. 21, 324, pp. 12b, 23b.

licence from the Prior or farmer omitted to perform it, the present grant was to be reckoned null and void. The seals of both parties were affixed to this agreement, which was dated as above.*

In an "Assembly" holden in the house of S. John of Jerusalem, at Clerkenwell, on the 20th of January, 1500-1, at which were present Brother John Kendal, Prior of England; Brother Henry Hawlay, Preceptor of Willughton; Brother Robert Pek, Preceptor of Badislay and Mayne; Brother Robert Dawson, Preceptor of Halston and Templecomb; Brother Thomas Newport, Preceptor of Newland; Brother Robert Danyel, Preceptor of Swynfeld; Brother Adam Chetwod, Preceptor of Badisford and Dynglay; Brother John Tonge, Preceptor of Ribston, Mount S. John, and Carbrok; Brother Jo. Bowth, Preceptor of Quenyngton; and Brother William Darel, Preceptor of Yeuelay and Barowe; a lease was granted to John Vernay of Farefelde, in the county of Somerset, esquire, of the Preceptory of Buclande Priors, in the county of Somerset, with the manors of Bodmescomb and Cove, in the county of Devon, appertaining to the said Preceptory, and all and singular other demesnes, lands, tenements, meadows, pastures, rents, services, contributions, courts with their profits, tithes, oblations, goods and chattels of felons and vagabonds, and all other liberties, emoluments, rights and advantages whatsoever; save and except woods and underwoods, advowsons of churches, guardianships, disposals in marriage, and admission fines, which were wholly reserved. The lease was to run from the festival of the Nativity of S. John the Baptist next coming, to the end of thirty years; and the rent to be paid into the Treasury at Clerkenwell was ninety-three pounds, six shillings, and eight pence sterling per annum,

* MS. Lansd. 200, f. lxxix b.

payable in equal portions at the festivals of the Purification of the Blessed Virgin and of S. Barnabas the Apostle. Besides this, the following stipulations (to us the far more interesting part of the transaction) were to be most strictly observed. The aforesaid farmer and his assigns were to provide due and honest hospitality in the Preceptory, at their own expence; and also, at their own expence, to find, according to the ancient order, five chaplains, two of whom, Chaplains of the Cross, or two others whom the Prior should depute, were to be assigned to places in the Church of the Sisters at Buclande, one in the Chapel of the Preceptory, one at Bodmescumbe, and one at Durston, for the continual celebration of Divine Service. They were also to find maintenance and a chamber for one chaplain of the Prioress, and maintenance for the steward of her House and for his servant, with two cartloads of hay, every year of the term. They were to give to Alexander Vernay, Chaplain of Bodmescomb, whose appointment we have already noticed, a chamber with his fuel there, and eight marcs sterling as stipend, and for his food and raiment, according to the tenor of the agreement previously made with him. Besides this they were to pay to the Prioress and Convent yearly for their customary pension the sum of £22, and to the steward of the courts pertaining to the said Preceptory his regular salary. Still further, they were to bear all other ordinary and extraordinary burdens incumbent on the Preceptory until the end of the term, the aids to the treasury at Rhodes excepted. They were to keep the buildings, walls, enclosures, hedges, &c., in good repair, and to return them in as sound a state as they received them. If any of the buildings should become ruinous during the term, the Prior was to rebuild them, and the farmer and his assigns were to repair and maintain them for the future. They were to find provision and attendance for three or four days and nights for the servants of the Prior coming with five or six horses twice a year on visitation to the said Preceptory, or for holding courts there. The aforesaid farmer and his assigns were to have housebote, fyrebote, ploughbote, cartbote, hedgebote, harobote, and foldebote, in and of the woods and underwoods of the said Preceptory by reasonable assignment and without waste. It was stipulated also that the Prior and his servants were to visit the said Preceptory whenever they pleased, and to hold courts and make leases; the farmer and his assigns to have the profits of the said courts, and to restore at the end of the term all the rolls of the courts, and leases, old and new, which should come to their hands during the interval. The farmer and his assigns were not to release their status in the Preceptory to any other holder without the licence of the Prior. If the rent went back, in part or in all, for two months after the dates above specified, it was to be lawful for the Prior to re-enter and take possession. If the profits of the contributions were suspended, the farmer and his assigns were to be allowed the difference, and to pay those monies only which they should actually receive. John Vernay bound himself to the performance of these agreements under a bond of two hundred pounds sterling; and also that at the end of the term he and his assigns should surrender to the Preceptor of Buclande all the ornaments of the chapel there, with all the stock living and dead. The document was signed with the seals of the Prior and of John Vernay aforesaid, and was "dated in our House of Clerkenwell, by London, in our Assembly holden there on the twentieth day of January, in the year of our Lord one thousand five hundredth."[*]

[*] MS. Lansd. 200, ff. lxxxiiii, lxxxiiii b. Appendix, No. XVIII.

It would appear either that this agreement was not observed, and that the alternative provided for came into operation, or that a transfer was effected with permission of the lessors; for so early as the 10th of March, 1507-8, at an "Assembly," holden on that day at the House at Clerkenwell, under the presidency of Thomas Docwra, Prior of England, assisted by Brother John Tong, Preceptor of Ribston, Mount S. John, and Carbrok; Brother Thomas Sheffeld, Preceptor of Bruerlay and Shengay; Brother Lancellot Docwra, Preceptor of Dynmore and Templecombe; Brother John Rawson, Preceptor of Swynfelde; and Brother Thomas Golyn, Preceptor of Baddisford and Dynglay, a lease of the Preceptory was granted to Edmund Myl, of Wellys, gentleman, and to Anna his wife, together with the manors of Bodmescomb and Cove, in the county of Devon. The terms of the lease are precisely similar to those already detailed, save that the special mention is omitted of Alexander Vernay, the Chaplain of Bodmescomb, who may be supposed to have departed this life during the interval.*

Once more a Confirmation was granted to the Sisters of their early privilege which has been so often before us. It is a document of a most curious kind, and especially so when we consider it with reference to the character of him from whom it came. In the second year of his reign, King Henry VIII. addressed letters of "inspeximus" to his beloved in Christ Thomas Docwra, Prior of the Hospital in England, recounting the terms of the previous letters, and granting through him to the Prioress and Sisters of Bucland a hundred and fifty-six cartloads of wood every year, from his park of Petherton, on the ground of their

---

* MS. Cott. Claud. E. VI. ff. liii b, liiii.

offering up constant and devout prayers for his own health and that of his dearest consort Katharine during their lifetime, and for their souls after their decease. Every cartload was to be of the draught of six horses or eight oxen; and, inasmuch as the time was limited in the former letters to the interval between the festival of the Annunciation and that of All Saints, they were now at liberty to collect the firewood from the latter festival to that of S. George the Martyr, the 23rd of April. They were also permitted to place sufficient fences round those parts of the park where the future fuel was growing, so that the young shoots might not be damaged, and that cattle and other animals might not injure the same. It was also allowed them, if they saw fit, to gather the amount of two years in one, but in that case they were not to remove any during the whole of the following year. All these concessions were to be enjoyed without any payment to the keeper of the park, or any fine to the hanaper of the chancery. The instrument was dated at Canterbury, 5th April, 1511.*

This arrangement was of but short duration. Edmund Myl died, and his widow became the wife of Lionel Norres in 1514. The lease was surrendered, and the Prior and his Chapter granted an annuity of ten pounds, out of the issues of the Preceptory, for the term of the life of the survivor. The instrument was dated the 11th of January, 1514-5.†

In 1516, the property was leased to Henry Thorneton, gentleman, of Currymalett, for forty years, from the festival of the Nativity of S. John the Baptist next ensuing, at a rent of one hundred and three pounds, six shillings, and

---

* Confirm. 2 Hen. VIII., p. 10, n. 7.
† MS. Cott. Claud. E. VI. ff. cxlvii, cxlvii b.

eight pence sterling a year. The increase of ten pounds in the yearly rental which is thus apparent was to meet the annuity of the same amount, just mentioned, which was, however, to revert to the farmer on the death of the annuitants. The terms of the lease in other respects were similar to those of the former. It was dated at the House of S. John at Clerkenwell, 24th April, 1516.*

It will be recollected that, by the conditions of the previous leases, there was an express reservation of the wood, underwood, and reparations of buildings. An indenture was made between Thomas Docwra, Prior of the Hospital of S. John of Jerusalem in England, and his brethren Knights of the same on the one part, and Henry Thornton, farmer of their Commandry of Bukeland, gentleman, on the other, by which the former covenanted, bargained, and sold for the residue of his lease unto the said Henry and his assigns all their wood and underwood lying, standing, and growing in their wood within the lordship of Hals, called Hals wood, containing by estimation 40 acres, save and except two trees of "oke" in the same wood, of the best "okes" that will and may serve for timber for the said Prior and his brethren, and their successors. For this concession the said Henry paid £20 sterling, with which the said Prior confessed himself to be well and truly satisfied and contented. It was agreed that the said Henry Thornton should repair and maintain at his own cost all manner of the houses and buildings; that it should be lawful for the said Henry to stub and grub all the said wood and underwood; and that he might, if he pleased, without impeachment of waste or destruction, alter, transpose and change such houses and buildings, provided that

* MS. Cott. Claud. E. VI., ff. clxii b, clxiii, clxiii b.

he made others in their stead. He bound himself and his heirs in the sum of £100 for the due performance of this engagement, which was entered into in the Chapter holden in the House of S. John's of Clerkenwell beside London, the 2nd of October, 1519.*

It should be remarked, that, although no mention is made in these documents of the Preceptor and his assistants at Buckland, we are not to conclude for certain, how likely soever, that such personages did not exist; because, according to the rule of the Order, as we have repeatedly noticed, they were simply officials, and the direction of their estates was virtually in the hands of the Superior at Clerkenwell. It would appear, nevertheless, that a change had taken place in the general mode of management. The position of the Preceptor and his Brethren, if such officers were still in being, which I hardly believe, was clearly very different from what it was when the accounts of their predecessors just two centuries before were so minutely laid open to our inspection.

On the same day as the date of the last instrument, the 2nd of October, 1519, the Prior and Chapter leased for a term of forty years, to the said Henry Thornton, farmer of Bucland, a tenement with its appurtenances, late in the tenure of John Curson, situated and lying in the parish of S. Clement Danes, outside Temple Bar. The rent was 40s. sterling a-year.†

We are now close upon times of trouble. I have already in previous Memoirs entered fully into the history of the unscrupulous movement which terminated in the violent suppression of the Religious Houses, and the wholesale

---

* MS. Cott. Claud. E. VI., ff. clxxxiiii, clxxxiiii b.
† MS. Cott. Claud. E. VI., f. clxxxviii.

robbery of their possessions. The main features of that odious tragedy are necessarily the same in every instance, although the details are as various as the multiform shapes in which tyranny, falsehood, sacrilege, and murder can present themselves and be exemplified when under no restraint nor necessity to deceive. Happily, therefore, there will not be any need to take the reader over ground with which he is already acquainted, and which is too unlovely to be voluntarily allowed to detain us. I will, accordingly, introduce him to the particular and special information which I have succeeded in gathering in connexion with the House on the history of which we are now employed.

Is is singular that no Declaration of the King's Supremacy, made either by the officers of the Preceptory or by the Sisterhood, has been preserved. It may be presumed that such was submitted to and accepted by them, but the record of the transaction is not extant.

Immediately afterwards, with a view to apportion the payment voted to the King for the support of his new dignity, followed the well-known "Valor." It is a most important document, as furnishing us with a minute account of the possessions of the House, with its income and expenditure in customary deductions, on the eve of the dissolution. I will, therefore, present the reader with its details, only more lucidly arranged than in their original and obscure form. Under each head he will thus be able without difficulty to see the gross and net values of the estates, both before and after the dues, stipends, and other disbursements had been accounted for and liquidated, and the subsequent surplus which remained for the maintenance of the House itself.

PRIORY OF MYNCHYN BOCKELAND.

Declaration of the Extent and Annual Value of all and singular the Lands and Tenements and other Possessions, with the Tithes, Oblations, and all other Issues of the divers Benefices and Chapels belonging and appropriated to the aforesaid Priory as below appeareth, namely in the time of Katerina Bowghshere, now Prioress at the same place, approved and examined by the Commissioners aforenamed [Sir Andrew Lutterell and Hugh Mallet, Esqr., Commissioners; Hugh Trotter and John Plompton, Auditors.].

LANDS ROUND THE PRIORY.

Value in issues of the Demesne Lands, remaining in the hands of the Prioress, and taxed by four trustworthy men. Thus clear } cxvij^s viij^d

BOOCKELAND.

Value in assessed Rents as well of the Free as of the Customary Tenants there, per annum .. xxij^{li}
Out of this, per annum,
For a chief rent there to the Prior of S. John of Jerusalem in England .. .. ix^d
So clear } xxj^{li} xix^s iij^d

Fines of land there .. .. .. xx^s

WELLYS.

Value in Rents of divers burgages there, per annum .. .. xlix^s
Out of this, per annum,
For rent to the Bishop of Bath .. ix^d
For the fee of William Vowell, steward there .. .. .. xiij^s iiij^d
For the fee of Alexander Pophame, bailiff there .. .. .. iij^s iiij^d
} **xxxj^s vij^d**
And there remains clear

GOTTON.

Assessed Rents as well of the Free as of the Customary Tenants there, per annum .. .. iiij^{li} xj^s
Out of which, per annum,
  For rent to the Abbat of Glastonbury .. .. .. xij^d
      And there remains clear } iiij^{li} x^s

NORTHPETHERTON.

Assessed Rents as well of the Free as of the Customary Tenants there, per annum .. .. xxiij^{li} ix^d
Out of which, per annum,
  For a priest in the parish church there, celebrating daily for the souls of Henry Erley and others, by agreement .. vj^{li} xiij^s iiij^d
  For the fee of John Walton, steward there .. .. xiij^s iiij^d
  For the fee of John Bckyn, bailiff there .. .. xxxiij^s iiij^d
      And there remains clear } xiiij^{li} ix^d

Fines of lands there, per annum xxx^s
Perquisites of the Courts and other Casualties .. .. iiij^s } xxxiiij^s

BRYMTON RAFF.

Assessed Rents there, per annum, clear .. xxiiij^s viij^d

CADECOTE.

Rent of one tenement there, per annum, clear ij^s iiij^d

HOREWOODE.

Rent of one tenement there, per annum, clear xiij^s iiij^d

Asshe and Thorneffawcon.

Assessed Rents there, per annum .. **xlvij^s vj^d**	}	
Out of which, per annum,		
For the fee of John Popham,	}	**xlv^s vj^d**
bailiff there .. .. .. **ij^s**		
And there remains clear		

County of Dorset.

Chyldcomb.

Assessed Rents there, per annum, clear .. **xiiij^{li}**

Pemeslegh in Shylborne.

Assessed Rents as well of the		
Free as of the Customary		
Tenants there, per annum **xiiij^{li} iij^s viij^d**	}	
Out of which, per annum,	}	**xiij^{li} ix^s iiij^d**
For rent to the Bishop of Sarum **xij^d**		
For the fee of John Hely,		
bailiff there .. .. **xiij^s iiij^d**		
And there remains clear		
Perquisites of the Courts there	}	
and other Casualties .. **iij^s iiij^d**	}	**xx^s**
Fines of lands .. .. .. **xvj^s viij^d**		

Value of Spirituals, as under.

County of Somerset.

Rectory of Bockeland with the Chapel of Midill Church.

Issues of predial tithes .. .. .. **vij^s xj^d**	}	
Of personal tithes.. .. .. .. **iij^s**	}	**xij^s v^d**
Other casualties there, in common years **xviij^d**		
Clear		

RECTORY OF KYLMERSDON.

Issues of predial and personal tithes xviij^{li} x^s
Demesne Lands, with other casualties
  there, in common years .. v^s
} xviij^{li} xv^s
  Clear

BROMEFYLD.

Issues of predial and personal tithes,
  demesne lands, with other casualties
  there, in common years .. .. viij^{li} v^s
Out of which, per annum,
  To the Archdeacon of Taunton, for
    synodals .. .. ij^s
} viij^{li} iij^s
  So clear

RECTORY OF NORTHPETHERTON.

Issues of predial and personal
  tithes, with other casual-
  ties there, in common
  years.. .. .. xxiiij^{li} x^d
Out of which, per annum,
  To the Bishop of Bath,
    for procurations .. ij^s iij^d
  To the Archdeacon of
    Taunton, for synodals vij^s v^d ob'
} xxiij^{li} xj^s j^d ob'.
  So clear

BRIGGEWATER.

A pension from the Prior there, for tithes of Horsy
  Mede, per annum. Clear .. .. .. viij^s

CANYNGTON.

A pension from the Prioress there, for tithes of
  Cleyhull, per annum. Clear .. .. .. vij^s

STONDENHAY.

A pension from Alexander Popham, for tithes
  there, per annum. Clear .. .. .. xl^s

COUNTY OF LINCOLN.

DYRTON.

Issues of tithes of all kinds .. xxix^{li}
Demesne Lands with other
 casualties, in common years xxij^s
Out of which, per annum,
For the fee of Gothlac Over-
 ton, the receiver there .. xxvj^s viij^d
Clear

} xxviij^{li} xv^s iiij^d

DONYNGTON.

Issues of tithes of all kinds, demesne
 lands, with other casualties, in
 common years .. .. .. x^{li}
Out of which, per annum,
For the fee of Gothlac Overton,
 the receiver there .. .. xiij^s iiij^d
Clear

} ix^{li} vj^s viij^d

ESSEX.

PRECEPTORY OF RAYNHAME.

A Pension paid by William Weston, Prior of S. John
 of Jerusalem in England, per annum. Clear .. c^s

SOMERSET.

PRECEPTORY OF TEMPLE COMB.

A Pension paid by Brother Edmund Husey
 there, per annum. Clear .. .. xxvj^s viij^d

KENT.

PRECEPTORY OF SWYNFYLD.

A Pension paid by Brother Edward Brown
 there, per annum. Clear .. .. xl^s

NORTHAMPTON.
PRECEPTORY OF KERDBROKE.
A Pension paid by Brother John Rawson there, per annum. Clear .. .. xiij^s iiij^d

KING'S ALMS.
Receipt by the hands of the Sheriff of Hereford yearly in the Exchequer of our Lord the King. Clear .. .. vj^{li} xiij^s iiij^d

SOMERSET.
CHURCH OF POWLET.
Annual Pension there. Clear .. .. .. xiij^s iiij^d

CHURCH OF NORTHPETHERTON.
Annual Pension there. Clear .. .. .. liij^s iiij^d

CHURCH OF TOLLANDE.
Annual Pension there. Clear .. .. ij^s

CHURCH OF BERYNTON.
Annual Pension there. Clear .. .. .. xx^s

TEMPORALS.
DEVON.
HELE, IN TAWSTOKE PARISH.

Assessed Rents as well of Free as of Customary Tenants, per annum, there .. xxiij^{li} xvj^s iiij^d q'	}	
Out of which, per annum,	} xxij^{li} xix^s viij^d q'.	
For the fee of Thomas Perd, steward there xiij^s iiij^d	}	
For the fee of Richard Payn, receiver there iij^s iiij^d	}	
And so clear		

Fines of lands there, per annum, .. xx^s
Perquisites of the Courts and other
    Casualties .. .. .. iij^s iiij^d
} xxiij^s iiij^d

CORNWALL.

BRODE WOODE WYGGER.
Assessed Rents as well of the Free as of the Customary Tenants there, per annum. Clear .. .. lxxv^s iiij^d ob'.

Sum total of the value as well of all the Temporals as of the Spirituals above mentioned .. .. ccxxiij^{li} vij^s iiij^d q'.
The tithe from thence .. .. .. xxij^{li} vj^s ix^d *

Such was the precise state and value of the property in the 27th year of Henry VIII., 1534.

The "Valor" gives us also the names of the following as Incumbents of benefices at the period of its formation :—

John Aisshelok was rector of Beckyngton, Thomas Thomson was vicar of Kilmersdon, Thomas Hill was vicar of Halse, John Dawes was rector of Hethfelde, Robert Balche was vicar of Powlet, John Bulcume was vicar of Northpetherton, John Langdon, Walter Jones and John Saunders were chantry priests in the same church, and John Crosse was rector of Tolland.†

This return confirmed the desires and paved the way for a carefully planned course of systematic aggression. Before, however, we enter into the narrative of the closing scenes, which are now rapidly drawing onwards, it will be best to dispose of a few particulars which would not be so well introduced in a subsequent page.

---

* Val. Eccl., vol. I., pp. 210, 211. MS. Harl. 701, f. 104b.
† Val. Eccl. I., 159, 160, 172, 212, 214, 223.

So far as we can learn from the details already presented, and I believe they are very nearly all that can now be recovered, the Sisters of Buckland, although constantly numbering in their community the daughters of great and noble houses, were but slenderly supported, and for a long time at least very far from adequately provided for. They were considered also in the light of a burden and grievance by the Officers charged in a special degree with their direction and general well-being. At first consisting, as it would seem, but of a Prioress and nine Sisters, the Society amounted in the year 1338 to so many as fifty ladies, who, together with their servants, must have needed a considerable revenue. No doubt but that a great part of the cost of their maintenance was defrayed, as the Preceptor then hinted in his return, by eleemosynary contributions from the neighbourhood and more distant friends. Their precise relationship to the Order of S. John has been, I think, greatly misunderstood. It has been said that they "had, at first, great dependance upon the knights, but afterward they disengaged themselves, and became a distinct Priory or Hospital of Nuns of the order of S. Augustine;"* and that "there is no mention of their being subordinate to any other Religious."† The contrary, as it appears to me, has been clearly shown. At no time were they distinct or independant. Their chaplain and steward were always officers of the Order; and they received their ancient pensions, and were accounted "obedientiariæ" down to the period of the Dissolution. That the Priory was distinct from the Commandry as a religious Community is, of course, certain; for it was the very reason of its foundation that the Sister-

---

* Tanner, Not. Mon. by Nasmith.   † *Ib.*

hood might be thus separated. But their union with the Order itself was never, that I can discover, broken. And the fact that they are called Nuns of the Order of S. Augustine is not to be understood as militating against this view, inasmuch as the Hospitalars, as well as the Templars, were members of that numerous body of Conventual Societies which accepted the rule of S. Austin as the guide of their religious life. Tanner's subsequent assertion that "it doth not appear when or by whom the Preceptory was founded, but some have thought it more ancient than the Nunnery," is so fully answered in the previous pages that it need not occupy us further.

Another and very conclusive evidence, at once of their obedientiary position and of their unbroken union with the Order, is exhibited in the fact that from beginning to end they did not so much as present to their appropriated rectories. I have recovered the following names of the incumbents of the parishes down to the time of the Suppression, and doubt not that, to the local reader especially, the lists, however imperfect, will be objects of considerable interest. It will be seen that the Prior of England, and neither the Prioress nor the Preceptor of Buckland, was the patron in every instance :—

Incumbents of North Petherton:—John de Messingham, 4th March, 1309-10; Laurence de Cherleton, 19th October, 1310; William de Dychton, 2nd August, 1313.* These were presented by Prior William de Tothale. Thomas de Foxtone, 6th September, 1332 ; presented by Prior Leonard de Tybertis. Nicholas de Somerton, 15th December, 1342; Nicholas de la Mor, 3rd October, 1345 ; William de Avene, 26th April, 1347; Reginald de Fardyngeston, 24th

* MS. Harl. 6964, pp. 10, 12, 51.

February, 1348-9 ;* presented by Prior Philip de Thame. John Harowe, A.M., 18th January, 1504-5; William Parkhowse, A.M., 8th June, 1523; presented by Prior Thomas Docwra. John Bulcombe, 30th October, 1531;† presented by Prior William Weston.

Incumbents of Kilmersdon : — William ———, 26th November, 1331 ; John de Messyngham, 6th January, 1334-5; presented by Prior Leonard de Tyberlis. John de Upton, 3rd August, 1341 ; Nicholas de Stanlak, 22nd August, 1348; John Markwille, 13th December, 1348 ;‡ presented by Prior Philip de Thame. Robert Symond, ———; Thomas Bourgchier, 14th September, 1521 ; James Harwode, 20th April, 1524 ; presented by Prior Thomas Docwra. Thomas Pullon, ———; John Tomason, (Thomas Thomson, of the "Valor") 17th June, 1534 ;‖ presented by Prior William Weston.

Incumbents of Elworthy:—John de Messingham, 19th October, 1310; William de Jarponnyle, 16th October, 1315 ; presented by Prior William de Tothale. Ralph de Hokynton, 24th November, 1323; Richard de Coute, 19th September, 1327;§ presented by Prior Thomas L'Archer. William Legh, 26th April, 1339; John de Sutton, 30th May, 1346 ; Walter de Chadleshounte, 28th August, 1349 ; John le Potter, 16th August, 1351; ¶ presented by Prior Philip de Thame. Stephen Chapman, ——— ; John Trevennaunt,15th March, 1455-6 ;** presented by Prior Robert Botyll. John Poole, ———; Edmund Sterne, 26th October,

---

* MS. Harl. 6965, pp. 61, 155, 173, 185, 203.
† MS. Harl. 6967, pp. 3, 42, 44b.
‡ MS. Harl. 6965, pp. 46, 84, 146, 191, 193.
‖ MS. Harl. 6967, pp. 29b, 34b, 47.
§ MS. Harl. 6964, pp. 12, 33, 84, 115.
¶ MS. Harl. 6965, pp. 126, 176, 219, 237.
** MS. Harl. 6966, p. 83.

1506 ; Robert Bailly, 5th May, 1509 ;* presented by Prior Thomas Docwra.

Incumbents of Halse :—Richard Philip, ——; Thomas Hyll, L.L.B., 23rd January, 1505-6 ;† presented by Prior Thomas Docwra.

Incumbents of Heathfield :—Owen de Cory, ——; Robert de Pippecote, 28th September, 1332 ; presented by Prior Leonard de Tybertis. Richard de Poterne, 4th July, 1346 ; Richard Payn, 22nd April, 1348; William Redmor, 4th February, 1348-9 ;‡ John de Donne, 1354 ; ‖ presented by Prior Philip de Thame. Thomas Banys, —— ; William Meyre, 10th March, 1505-6 ; presented by Prior Thomas Docwra. Edward Kebyll, ——; John Dawes, 2nd June, 1534 ;§ presented by Prior William Weston.

Incumbents of Tolland :—William de Banton, 20th January, 1265 ;¶ presented by Prior Roger de Vere. Gilbert de Quenton, ——; William de Quenton, 11th April, 1320 ;** William Morys, 28th August, 1349 ; Nicholas de Blenye, ——; Walter Stammel, 8th July, 1351 ; †† presented by Prior Philip de Thame. Walter Crosse, ——; John Crosse, A.M., 25th May, 1517 ;‡‡ presented by Prior Thomas Docwra.

It was doubtless for the peace of the Sisterhood that its members were so little called upon to interfere in the more secular affairs of their House. If power were less freely

---

* MS. Harl. 6967, pp. 6b, 11.
† MS. Harl. 6967, p. 5b.
‡ MS. Harl. 6965, pp. 64, 176, 180, 201.
‖ Hyll Cart. pp. 52, 53.
§ MS. Harl. 6967, pp. 5b, 47.
¶ MS. Harl. 6965 B., p. 121b.
** MS. Harl. 6964, p. 45.
†† MS. Harl. 6965, pp. 219, 236.
‡‡ MS. Harl. 6967, p. 23b.

imparted, we may hope that anxiety was removed in an equal measure. The maintenance of their rights was in stronger hands than their own; and the benefit was theirs without the labour and danger which its defence involved. The instance of the rector of Beckington is exactly in point. When the payment of his annual pension was not forthcoming, as we have seen, in the year 1353, the Prioress and Sisters had not to endure the ordeal of prosecuting their suit in person against the defaulter, but it was the great Prior of England who came to the rescue, and obtained the remedy which the law provided.

The daily life of these ladies in the privacy of their conventual home had, we may be sure, little to disturb its repose, save the occasional matters which we have had detailed, in which they were brought into contact with the noisy world without. They had little if any intercourse with the adjacent Commandry; as, in the first place, the statutes of the Order were imperative against the admission of women to domestic offices; and, in the second, the feeling existing between the two Societies was not such as to conduce to intimacies of a higher character. For the former position, indeed, their generally noble or gentle birth, and for the latter, their attitude, always, as would appear, antagonistic, equally disqualified them. Nor is there a single instance related of them (or I would have honestly mentioned it, as my object has invariably been to present as truthful an aspect as lies in my power of those Houses and their inmates whose chronicles I seek to rescue from oblivion), of any violation of the laws of morality. So far as we know—and we should be pretty sure to have some evidences of the contrary fact had it existed —the tongue of scandal itself was dumb. The blameless Sisterhood pursued its way of peace, broken only by trifling and unfrequent interruptions, or terminated by the end that comes alike to all. We may be well assured that the House was one of those, where, with all the religion, all the education of the age was encouraged, and where both religion and education yielded to the full their refined and refining influences. It was no doubt also a noted seminary for the daughters of the great neighbouring families. The Berkeleys, Erleghs, Montacutes, Wrothams, Bouchers and others were quite at home at Buckland, and learned from the good Sisters all the mental accomplishments which they in after life possessed. Reading, writing, some knowledge of accounts, the art of embroidery, music, and French, "aftur the scole of Stratford atte Bowe," was the recognised course of study; and we should wrong alike the teachers and the taught if we regarded the result as unfavourable. The life of intellectuality and religious quiet had many charms; and the pupil was doubtless so frequently enamoured of the contrast between it and that with which she was brought in contact elsewhere, that instances were not wanting of a resignation of all the worldly advantages that high birth and powerful connexions could impart to their possessor, and of a permanent abode as Sister or as Prioress within the venerable and well beloved walls of her early and holy home.

We have already noticed that, in the return made to the Grand Master of the Order in 1338, the Sisters are described as wearing the habit of the Hospital. The chief peculiarity of this consisted of a black mantle with a white cross in the front. In other respects the general attire of the ladies was, I presume, that of the members of Augustinian Sisterhoods—a black cloak with a long cowl, a short upper white tunic over a longer black one, and a whimple which covered the bosom and ascended in many folds to the chin.

I possess two interesting rings, which may be supposed to have decorated the fingers of more than one generation of the Sisters, and may indeed have been employed at the solemn ceremony which separated them for ever from the outer world and introduced them to the seclusion in which they sought and, we will believe, found repose. The earlier of the two is a work of the thirteenth century, and may so far have belonged to the good Prioress Fina herself. It is of gold, set with an unwrought sapphire, the hoop very thin and delicately engraved on the portions adjoining the stone. It was found in "Coglett Field," close to the site of the Priory, in 1858, by a labourer employed on the place. *(See the figure.)* The other, also of gold, but much stouter, is of the fifteenth century, and bears a heart on which is engraved the monogram ihs. It was found by another labourer in a field called "Broadworthy," near the site of the Priory, in 1853. *(See the figure.)* Another, which was described to me as of a cable pattern, was found in the immediate neighbourhood, in 1851, and has since been taken by its owner to one of our colonies.

No list of the Prioresses has hitherto been constructed. In the meagre accounts of the place already published, the name of the last only is given, and that but in connexion with the Dissolution and the events which almost immediately preceded it. Their succession is not recorded in the Episcopal Registers, and thus the best of all means of obtaining information of the names and dates of Superiors of Religious Houses is unfortunately in this instance of no avail. From all sources, however, I can at length supply the following series.

1. Fina, the first Prioress, who began her conventual reign in 1180, and died sixty years afterwards, in 1240.

2. Alianor de Actune (?) about 1280.
3. M——, previous to 1328.
4. Isabella la Louwe occurs in 1328.
5. Isabel de Berch occurs in 1330.
6. Katharine de Erlegh occurs in 1337.
7. Alicia occurs in 1405.
8. Katharine Bowser, Bowrghshere, Bourgeher, Bourgchier, Bourgheyr, Burgehier, Bourcher, or Boucher, the last Prioress, occurs in 1534, 1536, 1538, and 1539. The prominent facts in the life of this lady we shall shortly have before us in detail.

In this list I have not thought it necessary to enter into the circumstances connected with each of the Prioresses, as they have either been already given in the previous pages or will be presented to the reader before the conclusion of the History.

Collinson, from "MS. Palmer," says that Rachel Newton was Prioress in 1537, and that Elizabeth Carey and Catherine Nevil, Sisters of the House, were living in 1565, and married, the first to Thomas Speed, and the second to the Vicar of Ling. That these statements are entirely erroneous, I am able to prove by reference to the official list of the last members of the Sisterhood, which shall be given in its proper place, and wherein no such names appear. This must be held conclusive.

Of the Preceptors
1. John de Werewell occurs in 1320.
2. John Diluwe occurs in 1338.
3. Richard Marcis in 1536. This last I give on the authority of Collinson, who does not, however, add the source of his information, which may be as inaccurate and idle as the instance just before us.

My previous pages will supply the names of several

members of each Community at various periods of their history. To these the reader is referred.

Of the local features of the Priory and Preceptory we have no account save the incidental notices of various buildings in the Return of 1338, and a Survey mentioned by Collinson, from "MS. Palmer," as having been taken in the year 1571, when much of the conventual structure would have been altered if not totally destroyed. These notices relate exclusively to the Preceptory. In the former, as the reader will recollect, we have mention made of a court-house, a bakehouse, a dovecot, and a small church. The latter shows that the house "of the Preceptor and his brethren was on the north side of the great church," and was called at the period of the Survey "the House of the Lord Prior's steward." It must not, however, be inferred from this absence of detail that the Priory was otherwise than well fitted for its inmates. The religious Communities of the middle ages were usually occupants of structures of incomparable excellence, and we may be tolerably sure that such a Sisterhood as that of Buckland was no exception to this constant rule. Their abode was no doubt a picturesque group of buildings, to which nothing but the glorious architecture of mediæval times could have given existence; buildings ever lovely themselves, and attracting the love of all that look upon them with rightly appreciating and understanding eyes. It is much to be regretted that Leland who was in the immediate neighbourhood, if not at the very place, does not furnish us with a description of the scene. He pleasantly describes the park from whence the Sisters obtained their firewood, and the deer with which it abounded. "There ys a great Numbre of Dere longging to this (Pederton) Park, yet hath it almost no other Enclosure but Dikes to let [obstruct] the Catelle of the

Commune to cum yn. The Dere trippe over these Dikes & feede al about the Fennes, and resort to the Park agayn. There is a praty Lodge motid yn the Park There cummyth a praty Broke through the Park, and half a Mile beneth the Park it goith ynto Ivel. * * * * From the Lodge in Pederton Parke to Northpederton a Mile.* But he leaves the home of the Sisters without a word, and no care can now avail to supply its absence.

The Conventual Church was as usual a place of sepulture. It is true that we have but few visible evidences of the fact, though we still possess some which shall be subsequently described. I am happy, however, to perpetuate the testimony of an aged gentleman, whom I lately visited at Durston, and who kindly communicated his recollections of the place. He perfectly remembered the house belonging in his youth to the Lords Boringdon, which had been erected in the seventeenth century, with a noble hall of oak wainscot, "large enough to turn a coach and horses in." This he had himself helped to take down more than seventy years ago. Adjacent to it was an ancient chapel with a bell-gable, which was used for Sacred Service and in which he had been baptised, that shared at the same time the fate of the house. He remembered to have seen several monuments, with figures of men, some of them bearing shields on their arms. There were, so far as he recollected, no monuments of women; nor were there any ornaments, such as rings and the like, or money found during the alterations. Several hundred loads of stone were carted away, including some pieces of sculpture which were placed in a gentleman's garden at West Monkton. Thus much from my observant narrator. I was subsequently informed that

* Leland, Itin., vol. II., q. 66.

the gentleman alluded to was fond of decorating his grounds with relics from various localities; so that, if these objects yet exist, which I have been unable to discover, they could not be attributed to Buckland with any degree of certainty.

We will now take up the narrative from the point at which we left it.

On the 10th of December, 1534, Katherina Burgchier,* Prioress, and the Convent of Bokeland granted to John Popham, gentleman, the first and next advowson, donation, nomination, presentation or free disposition of the parish Church of Tolor, in the County of Dorset, whenever by death, resignation, deprivation, cession, or any other mode of avoidance, it should first and next chance to be vacant; the said advowson and presentation to be holden by the aforesaid John Popham and his executors and assigns for that one turn only. The Court of Augmentation confirmed this grant on the 20th of June, 1544.†

On the 31st of January, 1536, Katherina Boucher, Prioress, and her Sisters granted an annuity of £4 for life to John Tregunwell, doctor of laws, and one of the councillors of the most potent and dread king "potentissimi et metuendissimi regis" Henry VIII. It was to be paid in two equal portions, one at the festival of our Lord's Nativity, and the other on that of S. John the Baptist, and was stated to be in consideration of his counsel already and hereafter to be given.

* I scarcely need to remind the reader, who may be struck with the frequent variations in the orthography of proper names, that, throughout this and other Histories of Religious Houses, I invariably give them as they appear in the document which supplies the information then and there detailed.

† Orders and Decrees of the Court of Augmentation, vol. xiv., 2nd Nos. ff. 38b., 39.

I fear that this must be considered in the light of a bribe, or at best as a retaining fee for services which the receiver never intended to render, rather than for any valuable return either past or future. It was doubtless considered prudent to conciliate, as other communities did, the good will of a man of known and acknowledged influence, who might be of use in the troublous days on which the Religious Societies instinctively felt themselves to be entering. If the annuity were left unpaid for three months, the creditor had power to distrain on their lands in the county of Somerset. This grant was allowed by the Court of Augmentation, on the 11th of October, 1539, and ordered to be paid with the arrears from the time of the Dissolution.*

On the 10th of September in the same year, 1536, Katerina Bourgchier and Convent gave to Alexander Popham the office of Steward of their House or Hospital of Bokeland, with plenary authority in all matters appertaining thereunto, and also the profits and emoluments arising therefrom, together with an annuity of £4 of good and lawful English money, and one livery gown of the value of twenty shillings, or twenty shillings in lieu thereof. They also gave him the office of Receiver of all and singular the rents of their lands and tenements in Shirborne, in the county of Dorset, the duties to be performed either by himself or by a sufficient deputy, and an annuity of thirteen shillings and four pence, to be paid at Michaelmas during his life. If these sums remained unpaid for fifteen days, the said Alexander was empowered to enter and distrain on their lands in the parish of Northepetherton. The Court of Augmentation ordered the continuance of this annuity with arrears from the Dissolution, on the 7th of November, 1539.†

* Orders and Decrees, vol. VI., ff. clxxxix, clxxxix b.
† Orders and Decrees, vol. VI., ff. iiii^{xx}xiiii, iiii^{xx}xiiii b.

On the 1st of August, 1538, Katerina Bourgcher, Prioress, and Convent granted to the same Alexander Popham, for good counsel and faithful service, an annuity of six pounds thirteen shillings and fourpence, issuing from all their lands and tenements in the parish of Northpetherton, to be paid in equal portions at the feasts of Michaelmas, Christmas, Easter and S. John the Baptist. After non-payment for a month, he might enter and distrain on the lands in the parish of Northepetherton. This also, with arrears from the Dissolution, was ordered by the Court of Augmentation, on the same day as that of the previous order, the 7th of November, 1539.*

On the 1st of August, 1538, Katerina Bourgheyr, Prioress, and Convent granted to William Porteman, of Orchard, gentleman, in return for good counsel already and thereafter to be given, an annuity of twentysix shillings and eightpence, issuing from their manor of Northpetherton, and from all their lands and tenements within that parish, to be paid at Michaelmas. Here we have another instance of the extortions by submission to which the Religious Houses were obliged to secure the favour of the powerful, and also of the gross venality which characterized those who could without shame appropriate such infamous gains. No wonder that these were the men who soon afterwards were the foremost to struggle for the spoil. Non-payment for a month was to empower him to enter and distrain. This also was ordered to be continued for his life, together with arrears from the Dissolution, on the 4th of July, 1539.†

On the 2nd of October, 1538, an Indenture was made between " Dame Kateryn Bourcher, Priorisse of the House of Suster Buckland, and the Covent of the same House,

* Orders and Decrees, vol. VI, ff. iiii**xxvi, iiii**xxvi b.
† Orders and Decrees, vol. X., ff. iii^cxxxiiii b, iii^cxxxv.

of the one partye, and John Popham, gent., cytizen and haberdassher of London, of the other partye." This instrument, which, as the reader will have already perceived, is in English, sets forth, that, after the payment by the said John of a sum of twenty marcs sterling, the Prioress and Convent demised, granted, and let to farm all their parsonage of Kyrton, in the County of Lincoln, with all the glebe lands, and the tithes of corn, wool, and lambs, and all other profits of the said parsonage, the fourth sheaf paid to the lord Prior of S. John of Jerusalem always excepted and reserved. They also demised, granted, and let to farm the parsonage of Donnyngton, in the said County of Lincoln, with all the glebe lands, tithes, and profits of all kinds appertaining thereunto. These parsonages were let on a lease of forty years from the festival of the Nativity of S. John the Baptist next coming after. The rent was nine and thirty pounds sterling per annum, to be paid yearly at the festival of S. Barnaby the Apostle, that is to say, for Kyrton nine and twenty pounds, and for Donnyngton ten pounds. It was agreed to that the said John Popham should pay to the Vicar of Kyrton, every year at the feast of the Nativity of S. John the Baptist, the sum of four pounds seven shillings and seven pence: the Prioress and Convent to pay synodals and other claims due to the king and all other persons; and to maintain, sustain, and repair the said parsonages, houses, and walls at their own proper cost and charge. If the rent were not paid for the space of a quarter of a year, the Prioress and Convent might re-enter and expulse the said John and his executors and assigns. These terms were allowed and confirmed by the Court of Augmentation, on the 6th of November, 1539.*

* Orders and Decrees, vol. VI. ff. cviii. cviii b, cix.

The minuteness with which these and previous details have been presented to the reader will not be considered out of place or without value by any who desire to be acquainted with the state, habits and customs of ecclesiastical and civil England, as well as with the vicissitudes of this particular House, during the interesting period of the middle ages. They know that with this very minuteness much of the value and interest of researches like the present are necessarily associated. And for such students, I may add, my labours are intended.

It would appear that the family of Popham was benefitted in no ordinary degree by its connexion with the Priory. By a deed dated in their Chapter House, the 18th of January, 1539, Katherina Bourcher, Prioress, and Convent granted to Marmaduke Popham the office of Receiver of all and singular the rents of their Rectories of Kyrton and Denendon, in the County of Lincoln, the duties to be performed either by himself or by a sufficient deputy, with an annuity of forty shillings issuing from their lands and tenements at Premsleye, in the County of Dorset, to be paid at Michaelmas. On non-payment for a month after date, he was empowered to enter and distrain on their lands in Premsleye. The Court of Augmentation ordered the continuance of this annuity, with arrears from the Dissolution, on the 8th of November, 1539.*

This was the last official act that the Prioress and her Sisters performed previous to that involuntary one which placed all similar transactions at once and for ever beyond their power. The final blow was just about to fall, and but a brief respite yet awaited them. A short month elapsed and all was over.

* Orders and Decrees, vol. VI., f. 1.

On the 10th of February, 1539, the Chapter-house of Buckelonde was witness of the most melancholy scene that had ever been enacted within its walls. It was on that day that the Prioress and Convent were summoned to meet the Commissioners John Tregonwell and William Peter, and unwillingly affixed their conventual seal to the instrument of Surrender.* This was the conclusion of so much that piety and refinement had laboured at and brought to perfection, a conclusion whereof it is difficult to speak as its monstrous enormity deserves. The document still exists in the Record Office, with the impression of the seal appended. In the brief notice of this House by the last editors of the *Monasticon*, it is said that an impression had been seen by one of them, but so wholly flattened that no part of the subject of it could be discovered. This, if intended for the present, which I have every reason to believe, hardly gives a fair description of its state. The legend, indeed, belies its name, for it is illegible; but the device in the centre is clearly that of a Greek or Patriarchal Cross. *(See the figure.)* The form of the instrument itself is the one that was generally adopted, prepared as usual beforehand, and requiring merely the insertion of the name and style of the doomed House, and the signatures and seal of the pillaged inmates. In the case before us the signatures are wanting. It was, perhaps, too mournful a task and hard an effort for the unhappy Sisters to set their hands to a document which consigned them to everlasting exile from their ancient and beloved home. And, accordingly, the Commissioner John Tregonwell was fain to content himself with the subscription of his own name in the stead of other and better.†

* MS. Lansd. 97, f. 3b.
† Autograph. in Off. Record; Rymer, Fœd. xiv., p. 634.

I am able to furnish, from the unimpeachable authority of an original Pension List, the names and pensions of the entire Community who were witnesses of the ruin of their House. There were at the period of the Dissolution the Prioress and thirteen Sisters. Katheryn Bowser, Prioress, had a pension of £50 a year; Margaret Sydnam, subprioress, £4 13s. 4d.; Julyan Kendall, £4 6s. 8d.; Jone Hyll, £4; Anne Plummer, £4; Tomysyn Huntyngton, £4; Katheryn Popham, £4; Anne Maunsell, £4; Mary Dodyngton, £4; Ales Emerforde, £4; Jane Babyngton, £4; Mary Mathew, £4; Agnes Mathew, £4; and Isabell Grene, £4. There was also Priest William Mawdesley, confessor, and professed of their Order, who had a pension of £4. The document is signed :—Jo. Tregonwell, William Petre.* Dr. Archer says that the Prioress had also a gratuity of £25.†

In order to furnish all that we know of the subsequent history of these ladies, together with some notices of the officers and others, to whom, as we have already seen, orders were given for the continuance of their grants, I may add that in the year 1556 there remained charged upon the government the stipend of Alexander Popham, chief steward, 100s.; and annuities to—Alexander Popham, £6 13s. 4d.; John Tregonwell, £4; William Porteman, 26s. 8d.; and John Butler, 13s. 4d. Besides these, there were pensions to the following of the surviving Sisters. The orthography varies from that already given, but the persons can be easily identified. Johanna Hille, £4;‡ Thomasine

* Pensions, Hen. VIII. Miscell. Books, Off. Aug. vol. 245, n. 128. Appendix, No. XIX.
† E Reg. Fuller. 345.
‡ Not so much as a specimen of too frequent incorrectness, as of warning to those who perpetuate such by contenting themselves with simply copying the statements of others, I would mention the fate which this lady's name

Huntingdon, £4; Katerine Pophame, £4; Anne Maundefeld, £4; Johanna Bavington, £4; Elisabeth Grene, £4; and Agnes Mathewe, £4. And to William Maudesley, clerk, £4.*

John Andersey, the last Incumbent of the Chantry of Newton Placye, figures in the record as having an annual pension of 100s.; and Richard Verser, the last Incumbent of the Chantry of Blessed Mary in the Church of Northepetherton, as the receiver of an annual pension of the same amount.†

By a singular piece of good fortune, of which the history of no other Religious House that I know of can furnish an instance, we have thus had preserved for us the names of the first as well as the last Prioress and Sisters of Buckland—the former when brought together at the beginning from various Houses into one Conventual home; the latter both as they were at the evil day of their dispersion, and also when death had been busy among them after an interval of sixteen years. What became of these last during that interval, whither they betook themselves, and how they succeeded in bearing up under the anguish that memories of the happy past would scarcely fail to create, we know not. Nor can we gain more insight into their after fortunes. The notice just presented to the reader is the

---

has undergone. The scribe who copied the list for Willis wrote it "Llylbere," and thus it appears in the "History of Abbeys." (Vol. ii, p, 196.) Collinson has of course reiterated the assertion. The name in the original record is "Hille;" and the syllable added by the copyists is the first word of the "per annum iiii^{ll}" that follows! Many readers may consider this a matter of the most trifling consequence. It is an instance, however, which admits of too constant parallel; and the negligence which has given continuance to such errors is unworthy of the students of a branch of learning in which false statements are specially mischievous, and accuracy and exactness are of indispensible necessity.

* Card. Pole's Pension-book, f. xxix. Appendix No. XX.
† *Ib.,* fol. xxx.

concluding glimpse that we get of them. In subsequent records they appear no more.

We must now turn to the real cause of the hard measure and undeserved brutality so mercilessly dealt out to these innocent sufferers. The main temptation to the aggression against their peace was the lands with which ancient liberality had endowed them, and after which an unscrupulous tyrant and greedy courtiers thirsted, even to the robbery, or if need were, the murder of their lawful owners.

To illustrate the earliest condition of the property after it had been thus wrested from them and taken into the king's hands, I will furnish the reader with a brief but carefully made Abstract of the Return called the Ministers' Accounts, for the year ending at Michaelmas, 1539, the first, it will be remembered, subsequent to the Dissolution. The original record seems at the first aspect little less than obscurity itself, but this is to a great extent removed by adopting the tabular form in which it is here presented. The amounts have yet to be charged with sundry deductions in the shape of stipends, repairs, &c., as will be seen by comparison with the "Valor," where many of them are already given.

THE LATE PRIORY OF BUCKELOND.

THE ACCOUNTS OF ALL AND SINGULAR THE BAILIFFS, FARMERS, &C., FROM MICHAELMAS, 1538, TO MICHAELMAS, 1539.

THE ACCOUNT OF EDWARD ROGERS, ESQ., FARMER.
BUCKELOND.

Farm of the site of the late Priory, including gardens, orchards, and other lands, called xiiij Acres, Newlonde, Purches,

70   MYNCHIN BUCKLAND

Staplchays, Ryden, Robbys, Harys, Horlocke Mede, Hurt Mede, Longe Mede, vj Acres Mede, with their appurtenances, in the occupation of the said Farmer .. .. .. viij^{li} ij^s iiij^d
Farm of the Rectory .. .. xx^s
Sum total, ix^{li} ij^s iiij^d

THE ACCOUNT OF ALEXANDER POPPEHAM, BAILIFF.

HELE.

Assessed Rents .. .. xvj^{li} xiiij^d ob.
Farm of the Manor .. .. vj^{li} vj^s viij^d
Perquisites of the Courts .. iiij^{li} iiij^s viij^d
Sum total, xxvj^{li} xij^s vj^d ob.

THE ACCOUNT OF ALEXANDER POPPEHAM, COLLECTOR.

WELLYS.

Assessed Rent of one Burgage .. xx^s
Ditto of one Burgage .. .. xx^s
Ditto of one Burgage .. .. ix^s
Sum total, xlix^s

GOTTON.

Assessed Rent of one Messuage .. xl^s
Ditto of one Tenement .. . xl^s
Ditto of one Tenement .. .. v^s
Ditto of one Cottage .. .. vj^s
Sum total, iiij^{li} xj^s

BRYMTONRAFFE.

Rents of Messuage and Mill, with their appurtenances .. .. xxiiij^s viij^d

CADECOTE.
  Value of a tenement, late in the tenure of
    John Edwardes, ij^s iiij^d; but there
    were no returns, as it was not let.
HOREWOD.
  Chief Rent of a Mill .. .. xiij^s iiij^d
AYSSHE AND TORNFAWCON.
  Rents of lands, tenements, and cottages xlvij^s vj^d
BRODEWODWIGER.
  Rents of free Tenants .. .. x^s x^d
  Assessed Rents .. .. lxiiij^s v^d ob.
TOLLER.
  Farm of the Preceptory with Rectory xxij^{li}
S. JOHN OF JERUSALEM.
  Annual Rent received from the Prior,
    by ancient custom, but this year
    it was unpaid .. .. xxij^{li}
PERQUISITES OF THE COURTS. .. ix^{li}
    Sum total, lxviij^{li} ix^d ob.
    Remaining due, xxij^{li}

THE ACCOUNT OF THOMAS JESOPH, FARMER.
CHILCOMBE.
  Farm of the Manor .. .. xiiij^{li}

THE ACCOUNT OF RICHARD WAKEHAM, BAILIFF.
NORTHPEDERTON.
  Rents of free Tenants .. .. xxxiiij^s viij^d
  Assessed Rents .. .. xix^{li} ij^d
  Perquisites of the Courts .. xxx^{li} vj^s x^d
    Sum total, li^{li} xx^d

THE ACCOUNT OF ALEXANDER POPPEHAM, BY JAWCUS AYSSHELEY, HIS DEPUTY.

PRYMSLEY.

 Rents of free Tenants .. .. xj^s iiij^d
 Assessed Rents .. .. xiij^{li} xij^s vj^d
  Sum total, xiiij^{li} iij^s x^d

THE ACCOUNT OF ALEXANDER POPPEHAM, FARMER.

KYLMERSTON.

 Farm of the Manor with Rectory .. xviij^{li} xv^s

THE ACCOUNT OF JOAN ATWYLL, FARMER.

BROMFYLD.

 Farm of the Rectory .. viij^{li} v^s

THE ACCOUNT OF JOHN WORTH, GENT., BY ALEXANDER POPPEHAM, HIS DEPUTY.

NORTHEPEDERTON.

 Farm of the Rectory .. .. xxvj^{li} x^d
 Pension from the Vicarage .. liij^s iiij^d

PAWLETT.

 Pension from the Vicarage, this year unpaid xiij^s iiij^d
  Sum total, **xxix^{li} vij^s vj^d**
  Remaining due, xiij^s iiij^d

THE ACCOUNT OF MARMADUKE POPPEHAM, RECEIVER.

KYRTON.

 Farm of the Rectory .. .. **xxix^{li}**
 Rent of three cottages, parcel of the
  aforesaid .. .. **xxij^s**

DONYNGTON.

 Farm of Tithe, &c. .. **x^{li}**
  Sum total, **xl^{li} ij^s**

PRIORY AND PRECEPTORY. 73

The Account of Alexander Poppeham, Collector.

Rayneham, in Berks.
Pension from the Preceptory, this year unpaid   c^s

Swynfild, in Kent.
Pension from the Preceptory, this year unpaid   xl^s

Kerbroke, in Northamptonshire.
Pension from the Preceptory, this year unpaid   xiij^s iiij^d

Templecome, in Somerset.
Pension from the Preceptory, this year unpaid xxvj^s viij^d

Toland, in Somerset.
Pension from the Rectory   ..   ..   ij^s

Bekyngton, in Somerset.
Pension from the Rectory   ..   xx^s

Sheriff of Hereford.
A certain Alms of the King, this year unpaid vj^{li} xvj^s xj^d

$$\text{Sum total,} \quad \text{xvj}^{li} \text{ xviij}^s \text{ xj}^d$$
$$\text{Remaining due, xv}^{li} \text{ xvj}^s \text{ xj}^d \text{ *}$$

On a comparison of these accounts with those already given in the "Valor," it will be found that very little difference exists between them. Indeed, in more than half the cases, the values given are identical.

Such was the spoil. We have now, in conclusion, to see how it was disposed of, and who were the richer for the transfer.

The first notice that we have of the use to which the revenues were devoted may be considered the least objectionable of the whole. On the 27th of February, 1540, the king granted to John Worth, Esq., an annual pension of £24

---

* Ministers' Accounts, 30-31 Hen. VIII. Off. Aug.

and 10d., issuing from the manor of Bucklond, formerly belonging to the late Monastery of Bucklond, just now dissolved. We have already seen this John Worth in the character of Receiver of rents and pensions from Northepederton and Pawlett.*
Some time elapsed before the bulk of the property was disposed of. A "Request to purchase" the site of the Priory and the Rectory and tithes of Mighelchurch was submitted to the king, signed "W. Essex," and bearing date the 11th of March, 35th Hen. VIII., 1544. To the enumeration of the various portions of the domain, which will presently be detailed in the grant, the Auditor, Mathew Coltehirste, whose duty it was to examine the terms of the Request, and to report upon any charges on the estates, appended the following note.† — " What comoditie the ffermer hereof taketh aboue the annual Rent I knowe not. It'm the kynges grace is charged wth evj^s viij^d for the stipend of a preeste serving Cure at Sancte Michaell Chapell being w'in a q'rter of a myle of the seid seite. where they wedde & crisen & burith in the Churche Yarde of the seid late Pryory. & so is like to be charged. vnlesse the seid Chapell be annexed to the Chapell of a Comoundry of Sancte Johnes adionyng to the seid seite: there is no more landes w'in ij myles perteynyng to the seid *Priory.* the Comaundry of Bucklande parcell of Sancte Jones adioneth to the same. P'Mathiam Coltehirste Audit'." In the margin we are told that "The superfluous howsys there where sold to the seid ffermer [Edward Rogers] at the tyme of the dissolucyon of the howse." The woods on the estate are reported as follows:—Roden Coppies, 3

---

* Carlæ Miscell. in Off. Rec. vol. 7, n. 28.
† Part. for Grants, Off. Aug. The letters printed in italics are represented in the original by marks of contraction.

acres; Wynsell Wood, 7 acres; and hedgerows, 2 acres; with sundry reservations for the farmer of the demesne.*

This was shortly afterwards followed by the instrument which the framers had in view. On the 30th of June, 1544, the king granted to his beloved and faithful cousin and councillor, William, Earl of Essex, and his beloved James Rokeby, Esq., William Ibgrabe, Esq., and John Cokke, Edward Rogers, and Edward Bury, Esqrs., and their heirs, &c., for the sum of £1049 11s. 2½d. of lawful money of England, the whole House and Site of the late monastery of Buckland, in the County of Somerset, and all its lands, meadows, pastures and hereditaments, called or known by the name or names of Fouretene Acres, Newland, Purches, Staplcheys, Riden, Lobbis, Harys, Horlocke Meade, Hurte Meade, Longe Meade, and Sixe Acres Meade, with all their appurtenances, then or lately in the tenure or occupation of the said Edward Rogers or his assigns, in Bucklande, or Buckland Sororum, parcel of the possessions of the said late monastery, and formerly in the hands, culture, and proper occupation of the late Prioress of the late monastery of Buckland at the time of the Dissolution. Also all those woods and lands called Riden Coppes and Wynsell Wood, containing by estimation ten acres, with all their appurtenances in Buckland. Also all the houses, buildings, granaries, stables, dovecots, gardens, orchards, and lands whatsoever, within the site, sept, boundary, circuit, and precinct of the said late monastery, and all and singular commons, ways, paths, easements, advantages, profits, and emoluments whatsoever in Buckland, Mighelchurche, and Northpetherton, in any manner appertaining. Also all the Rectory, and church, or chapel of Mighelchurche, with its appurtenances; and all and every kind of tithes of green crops, corn, grain, hay, wool, lambs,

* Part. for Grants, Off. Aug.

and other small tithes, and oblations, revenues, and profits whatsoever in Mighelchurche and Buckland, in any way appertaining to the said Rectory, and Church or Chapel of Mighelchurche. All these were to be holden as fully and entirely as the last Prioress had them. The aforesaid site, and lands, and properties of various descriptions were stated to be of the clear annual value of seventy-five shillings and eightpence. They were to be held of the king in chief, by the service of a twentieth part of one knight's fee, and an annual rent of seven shillings and sevenpence sterling, to be paid at Michaelmas. The grantees were also to pay one hundred and six shillings and eightpence a year for the stipend of a curate to celebrate Divine service in the Church or Chapel of Mighelchurche. Besides all this the grant conveyed enormous possessions in the parishes of S. Botolph, Aldersgate, S. John, Clerkenwell, and S. Sepulchre, in the city of London and county of Middlesex, and in the counties of York, Northumberland, Stafford, Hertford, Wilts, and Essex. The instrument was dated at Westminster, on the day and year above mentioned.*

On the 13th of October, 1544, in consideration of the sum of £754 17s. 8d., of good and lawful English money, the king granted to William Porteman, Sergeant-at-Law, and Alexander Popham, Esq., and their heirs, &c., all the manor of Northpetherton, or Northpederton, with all and singular its rights and appurtenances, formerly belonging to, and parcel of the possessions of, the late dissolved Priory of Bukland, and all the site, demesne lands, meadows, pastures, &c., of the said manor. Also the wood commonly called Darwoods, in Northpetherton, containing by estima-

* Orig. 36 Hen. VIII. p. 1. rot. xxxviii. Pat. 36 Hen. VIII., p. 2, mm. 34 (13), 33 (14), 32 (15), 31 (16). Leland, Itin., vol. II., p. 68. Appendix, No. XXI.

tion eight acres. Also all the messuages, lands, tenements, meadows and pastures, with their appurtenances, in Gotton, in the parish of Westemonketon, formerly belonging to the late Priory, in the tenure or occupation of Richard Warr, Esq., Robert Warr, William Hare, and Weltheane Merkes, widow. Also all the messuages, tofts, houses, buildings, granaries, stables, dovecots, mills, gardens, orchards, meadows, woods, waters, marshes, vivaries, weirs, fisheries, commons, wastes, &c., &c., with all knights' fees and other rights, in Northpetherton, Michelchurche, Bromfeld, Brympton Raiff, Wollavyngton, Mirclinche, and Gotton—as fully and entirely as Katerina Bourgchier the last Prioress had held the said property. Also messuages, &c., in Ayshe and Thornfaucon, lately belonging to the said Priory. Also a tenement and messuage in the parish of Bromefeld, formerly belonging to the lately dissolved Priory of Taunton, in the occupation of one Richard Raynald. Also another tenement and messuage in Bromefeld, in the tenure and occupation of one John Pylman, formerly belonging to the late Priory of Taunton. Also lands in Kyngeshyll, in the parish of Spaxton, also formerly belonging to the late dissolved Priory of Taunton. Also all the manor, farm, and grange of Claveshey, with its appurtenances, in the parishes of Northepetherton and Bromefelde; and the capital messuage, house, site, and capital mansion of Claveshey, formerly belonging to the lately dissolved monastery of Athelney; and the wood commonly called Claveshey Wood, containing by estimation ten acres, and the wood called Holesey Wood, containing by estimation five acres, in Northepetherton aforesaid, formerly belonging to the late monastery of Athelney. Also messuages, &c., at Durlegh, Gotchirst, Dunwer, &c., in the parishes of Bridgewater and Northepetherton, formerly belonging to the

Priory of S. John, at Bridgewater. The property formerly belonging to the Priory of Buckland in Buckland, Northpetherton, Michelchurch and Bromefeld, was estimated at the clear annual value of £23 17s. 4d.; in Ayshe and Thornefaucon, of 47s. 6d.; at Bromefeld and Spaxton, of 41s. 8d.; at Claveshey, of £9; at Durleigh and Gotchirst, of 33s.; and at Dunwer, of 14s. 6d. The grantees were to pay the following annual rents :—for the property at Buckland, 38s.; for Gotton, 9s. 1½d.; for Ayshe and Thornfaucon, 4s. 9d.; for Bromefeld and Spaxton, 4s. 2d.; for Claveshey, 18s.; for Durlegh and Gotchirst, 3s. 4d.; and for Dunwer, 17½d. Also to Richard Wakeham, bailiff of the manor of Northepetherton, an annual fee of 20s.; and to John Walton, steward of the court of the said manor, 13s. 4d. All advowsons of churches, and spiritual emoluments and profits were reserved to the king. The Request to purchase was dated the 6th of July, 1544; and the grant at Westminster, the 13th of October, in the same year.*

We have already seen the disposal of the Priory, and have now to notice that of the Preceptory, which was not long delayed. The Request to purchase is dated the 13th of December, 1544. Ralph Lambe, the deputy of Matthew Coltchirste, Auditor, annexed to the enumeration of the lands thus solicited the significant and not unusual declaration, "I have made the particlers hereof to no other person, nor I knowe any other person desyrus to bye the premysses."† This was doubtless intended to assure the royal salesman that the bargain was the best that could be effected under the circumstances. On the 16th of

---

* Part. for Grants, Off. Aug. Orig. 36 Hen. VIII., p. 3, rot. xii. Pat. 36 Hen. VIII., p. 8, mm. 23, 24, 25, 26. Add. MS. B.M. 6366, pp. 28 b, 29.

† Part. for Grants, Off. Aug. Appendix, No. XXII.

February, 1545, the purchase was completed. The king then granted to Alexander Popham, Esquire, and William Halley, gentleman, and their heirs, &c., in consideration of the sum of £999 16s. 7d. of lawful English money, all the manor and the late Preceptory of Buckland Pryours, in the County of Somerset, together with the manor of Halse, and all other manors, lands, tenements, meadows, pastures, rents, reversions, services, and other hereditaments whatsoever, appertaining to the said late Preceptory, with all its other members and appurtenances, then or lately in the tenure, discharge or occupation of the aforesaid William Halley. Also the Rectory and impropriated Church of Halse, and all and singular other Rectories and impropriated Churches appertaining to the said Preceptory ; and all glebes, tithes, pensions, portions, oblations, revenues, fruits, advantages, profits, emoluments, and hereditaments whatsoever, as well spiritual as temporal, of every kind. Also the advowsons and rights of the Rectories aforesaid. Also the two manors of Bodmescombe and Cove, in the County of Devon, with all their appurtenances. Also the manor of Cleyanger, in the County of Devon. Also the advowsons, donations, presentations, &c., of the Church and Rectory of Hethefeld, and of the Church and Rectory of Halse, in the County of Somerset ; and of the Rectories and Churches of Brendon and Cleyanger in the County of Devon. Also the wood and grove called Wynsell Grove, containing by estimation four acres; and the wood and grove called Peryfeld Grove, containing by estimation four acres ; and the grove called Bowyers Grove, containing by estimation twelve acres ; and the wood and waste called Bodmescombe Wood, containing by estimation thirty-five acres; and twelve acres, sixteen acres, and twenty-seven acres, called Uprynges of Wood ; all parcels of the late Preceptory of

Bucklond Pryours. Also a messuage, &c., in the parishes of Gotehurste and Charlinche, formerly belonging to the late Priory or Hospital of S. John of Brydgewater. Also the demesne and manor of Thurlebare; the messuage, &c., called Playstrete, in the parish of Staple; a rent of twenty-four shillings and ninepence half-penny, called The Thurchetts,* issuing from certain lands and tenements in Thurlebare; a close called The Pryours Wood, in Thurlebare, of thirteen acres; and lands in Westhatche and Upphatche; all formerly belonging to the late Priory of Taunton. Also the manor and demesne of Tobrydge, with all its rights, &c., in the parish of S. James by Taunton, and formerly belonging to the late Priory of Taunton. All these were to be holden by the grantees as fully, entirely, and amply, as by their former possessors. The manor and late Preceptory of Buckelond Priours together with the manor of Halse, &c., were of the clear annual value of £31 19s. 2d., without deducting the reserved tithe; the vicarage of the clear annual value of £5 19s. 5½d., without deducting the reserved tithe; and the Rectory of Hethefeld, £9 4s., without deducting tithe. The Preceptory of Bucklond Pryours and Halse were to be held by the grantees of the king in capite, by military service, to wit, the twentieth part of one knight's fee, and by the following annual rents, to be paid at Michaelmas:—for Buckelond and Halse, £3 3s. 11d.; for Tobrydge, 10s. 7d.; for Cleanger, &c., 10s. 2d.; and for Thurlebare, 14s. 5d. The grant was dated at Westminster, the 16th of February, 36 Hen. VIII., 1544-5.†

* Probably intended for Churchetts, or Churchessels, a payment to the Church of corn as the First-fruits of harvest. See, for another instance, the author's History of Taunton Priory, page 119.

† Orig. 36 Hen. VIII., p. 8, rot. xvii. Pat. 36 Hen. VIII., p. 26, mm. (6) 41, (7) 43, (8) 42. Add. MS. B.M. 6366, p. 116. Appendix, No. XXIII.

PRIORY AND PRECEPTORY. 81

The more distant portions of the property were disposed of in a similar manner.

On the 18th of July, 1543, in consideration of the sum of £1451 2s. 9¼d., the King granted to Sir John Horsey the manor of Prymsley, or Promsley,* in the county of Dorset, with all its rights, members, and appurtenances, formerly belonging to the late dissolved Priory of Buckelande, in the County of Somerset. Together with this were granted lands at Thorneforde, Overcompton, and Nethercompton, and at Pynford, in the parish of Shirborne. Prymsley was estimated at the clear annual value of £14 17s. 2d. The lands were to be held of the King in capite, and the annual rent for Prymsley was to be the sum of 29s. 9d., payable at Michaelmas. The Request to purchase was dated the 5th of June, 1543; and the grant at Terlynge, on the day above mentioned.†

One month after a Request to purchase, dated the 6th of July, 1543, the King granted to Richard Parker, of Tawstok, in the County of Devon, gentleman, for the sum of £1436 7s. 10d., the Rectories of Bradford and Hilfaraunce, in the County of Somerset, formerly belonging to the Priory of Barliche; the demesne and manor of Pyxton, and Nynched, formerly belonging to the Priory of Taunton; the manor of Morenialcherbe and Brodewodwiger, in Devon, formerly belonging to and parcel of the late Priory of Mynchyngbukland, in the County of Somerset; the Rectory of Northemolton, and lands at Lynkcombe, Hilfarcombe, and Wykelangforde, &c., formerly belonging to the late Monasteries of Dunkeswell and Frythelstoke, in the County of Devon. Bradford and Hilfaraunce were

* See page 13 for the original gift.
† Part. for Grants, in Off. Aug. Orig. 35 Hen. VIII., p. 2, rot. iiii. Pat. 35 Hen. VIII., p. 6, mm. (1) 38, (2) 37.

L

of the clear annual value of £16 4s. 6d.; Pyxton and Nynehead, £15 15s.; Lynkcombe and Hilfarcombe £12 7s. 0½d.; Northemolton, of £16; and Moremalcherbe, £3 15s. 3½d. The advowsons were reserved. The property was to be held in capite, by the service of a twentieth part of one knight's fee, and the following annual rents to be paid at Michaelmas:—for Bradford and Hilfaraunce, 32s. 5½d.; for Pyxton, &c., 31s. 6d.; for Lynkcombe, 24s. 8½d.; for Northmolton, 32s.; and for Moremalcherbe, 7s. 6½d. Besides these charges, the grantees were to pay annually to the Curate of Hylfaraunce a stipend of 26s. 8d.; for procurations and synodals for the Church of Bradford, the sum of 12s. 5½d.; to the bailiff of Lynkcombe, his fee of 13s. 4d.; to the Vicar of Northemolton, £17 6s. 8d.; and, lastly, the sum of 66s. 8d., for the said Rectory of Northemolton, to the Dean and Chapter of the Cathedral Church of S. Peter at Exon. The grant was dated at Rayne, the 6th of August, 1543.*

On the 11th of June, 1544, the King granted to Sir John Fulford, Humfrey Colles, Esquire, and their heirs, certain tenements with their appurtenances in the parish of Bromfeld, in the tenure or occupation of Robert Stalyche, John Harle, and John Hewett, formerly belonging to the late Priory of Bukeland. Also a horse mill, and a moiety of a close called Newe Close, and five acres of meadow with their appurtenances in Rysemore, in the County of Somerset, in the occupation of John Grene and Johanna his wife, and formerly belonging to the late Hospital of S. John of Bridgewater. Lands in Devon, formerly belonging to the late monasteries of Canonleighe,

---

* Part. for Grants, in Off. Aug. Orig. 35 Hen. VIII., p. 1, rot. cxvii. Pat. 35 Hen. VIII., p. 5, mm. 12 (26), 11 (27), 10 (28). Add. MS. B.M. 6365, p. 297.

S. Nicholas at Exon, and Buckfast, in that County, and of Mountague and Clyve, in the County of Somerset, accompanied the aforesaid, and the purchase money amounted to the sum of £1199 18s. 3d. The property belonging to Bukeland was estimated at the clear yearly value of 24s. 4d., the tithe not deducted ; and that belonging to S. John of Bridgewater to £4, the tithe also not deducted. The grantees in capite were to pay, at Michaelmas, for the Bridgwater property the yearly rent of 8s.; and for that at Bromfeld 2s. 5¼d. The Request to purchase was dated the 12th of March, 1544; and the grant at Westminster on the day aforesaid.*

On the 26th of July, 1544, (the Request is dated the 10th of the same month,) the King granted to Roger Taverner and Robert Taverner, gentlemen, two tenements and a mill called Elsam Myll, and certain lands and tenements called Stone Londes, situated in Brompton Raffe, in the County of Somerset, with all their appurtenances, in the tenure or occupation of John Edwardes, and formerly belonging to the late dissolved Priory of Buckelonde, in the said county. The annual value was 24s. 8d.; and it was to be held by a yearly payment, at Michaelmas, under the name of tithe, of 2s. 6d. This was accompanied by large estates in London and the Counties of Northampton, Lincoln, and York, and the amount paid for the whole was £546 17s. 6d. The grant was dated, witness Katharine Queen of England, at Westminster, on the day and year aforesaid.†

On the 8th of November, 1544, a year which witnessed such wholesale changes in the possession of Church property, the King, in consideration of the sum of £269

* Part. for Grants, in Off. Aug. Orig. 36 Hen. VIII., p. 4, rot. clxvi. Pat. 36 Hen. VIII., p. 12, mm. 5 (35), 4 (36), 3 (37).

† Part. for Grants, in Off. Aug. Orig. 36 Hen. VIII., p. 5, rot. iii.

13s. 4d., granted to William Bisshoppe, of Bredy, in the County of Dorset, yeoman, and to John Hide, of London, gentleman, and their heirs, the manor of Chylcombe, with all its rights, in the County of Dorset, lately belonging to the Priory of Buklande.* Also other lands in Southampton, &c. The clear annual value of Chylcombe was reckoned at £14. It was to be held of the King in chief, by payment of a yearly rent of 28s. at Michaelmas. The Request to purchase was dated the 8th of November, 1544; and the grant at Westminster, on the day above mentioned.†

On the 13th of the same month they obtained license, we are told, to alienate a moiety to Thomas Martin, of Longbridy, and his heirs. William Bisshoppe did not long enjoy his new estate. He died on the 31st of May, 1545, leaving the ominous property to his son John, who succeeded his father at the age of seventeen years, and died four years after, 3 Edward VI! ‡

Nine months elapsed before other changes were effected. On the 4th of July, 1545, the King granted to William Hodgys, of Myddelchynnock, in the County of Somerset, and to William Hodgys, of London, son of the former, and their heirs, for the sum of £695 0s. 5d., the site of the Monastery of the Grey Friars of Ivellchester, twenty-nine messuages in the town of Bridgewater, lately belonging to the Hospital of S. John in that town; and three messuages or burgages in the city of Wells,|| in the separate tenure or occupation of Thomas Bodye, Cristofer Cooke, and Leticia Trystes. To these were added other lands in the counties of Dorset and Derby.

* See page 13 for the original gift.
† Part. for Grants, in Off. Aug. Orig. 36 Hen. VIII., p. 4, rot. ciiiixxi.
‡ *Hutchins's Dorsetshire*, 2nd Ed., vol. II, p. 293.
|| See page 19 for the original gift.

PRIORY AND PRECEPTORY. 85

The property in Ivelchester was reckoned of the clear annual value of 13s. 4d.; that in Bridgewater, of £21 3s. 4d.; and that at Wells, of 49s. It was to be held by fealty, in free soccage, and not in capite. The Request to purchase was dated the 24th of February, 1545; and the grant as above, at Westminster.*

The spoil was not yet entirely disposed of. For the sum of £1393 8s. 10d., the King granted to John Pope, gentleman, and his heirs, the manor of Kyrton in Holland, in the County of Lincoln, lately belonging to Buckland Priory, with all its houses, lands, and other appurtenances, of the clear yearly value of 22s. An enormous tract in the Counties of Oxford, Gloucester, York, Wilts, Salop, Middlesex, Surrey, and Warwick accompanied the aforesaid property. Kyrton was to be held in free soccage, by fealty only, and not in capite. The Request to purchase was dated the — day of July, 1545, and the grant at Westminster, the 3rd of October, 1545.†

By this time, as the reader will have perceived, not much remained either to excite or to gratify the lust of acquisition. My task, accordingly, is all but completed. Of course I cannot pursue further the history of each estate, which has now ceased to be of the interest that it hitherto possessed. The exception, however, which I have made in previous instances, it will not be improper to repeat in this.

So early as four years after the original grant to William Halley, in whose occupation, it will be remembered, the property even then was, King Edward VI., in consideration of the sum of £6 13s. 4d., authorized him to alienate to John Cuffe and John Tynbery, and their heirs,

* Part. for Grants, in Off. Aug. Orig. 37 Hen. VIII., p. 6, rot. xxx.
† Part. for Grants, in Off. Aug. Orig. 37 Hen. VIII., p. 3. rot. xvi. Pat. 37 Hen. VIII., p. 3, mm. 13 (33), 12 (34), 11 (35), 10 (36), 9 (37).

his capital messuage called Buckclond Priors, with its appurtenances, and two gardens, two orchards, two hundred acres of arable land, thirty-six acres of meadow, seventy-three acres of pasture, and two acres of land covered with water—the Ponds, I presume, to which I drew attention in the beginning of the History—with their appurtenances, in Buckland Priors and Coglod, in the County of Somerset, holden of the King in capite. Also to the aforesaid John Cuffe and John Tynbery special license was given to appropriate the same. The grant was dated at Westminster, the 13th of February, 1548.*

On the 4th of July, 1608, Edward Rogers, son of George Rogers, of Canington, sold to Sir Henry Hawley the site, circuit and precinct of the late Monastery or Priory of Buckland, with its appurtenances.† The manor, according to Collinson,‡ was subsequently sold by the Hawleys to John Baker, Esq., Receiver General of the land-tax in the County of Somerset, whose son Christopher sold it to George Parker, of Boringdon, in the County of Devon, Esq., and his decendant, John Parker, Baron Boringdon, to the family of the present possessor.

Thus have we traced the history of this interesting spot, from its original selection for the abode of a Religious Community, through ages of dutiful attention to the grand objects for the advancement of which it was so chosen, of varying fortune and frequent struggle, down to its violent alienation from those objects and its compulsory separation from the Society with which they were con-

* Orig. 2 Edw. VI. p. 1. rot. xlv. Pat. 2 Edw. VI., p. 1, m. (11) 35. Add. MS. B.M. 6367, f. 30. Appendix, No. XXIV.
† Trin. Rec. 9 Jac. i. rot. cxii.
‡ Vol. III. p. 99.

nected. The present appearance of the place gives very little indication of the former of these associations. Various fragments, indeed, of an older structure, as plinth mouldings and similar remains, are noticeable in the more ancient of the farm buildings, and there still exists a barn with some buttresses of the late Perpendicular period. Nothing, however, that I noticed, connected with the structure itself, is necessarily earlier than the sixteenth century, and accordingly all that is now visible may have formed no part of the conventual edifices, but have been the work of the first intruders to accommodate the place to their own purposes. Apart from the Ponds, already described, there are nevertheless a few relics of monastic days, which I have had the happiness of bringing into notice. This has not been effected without some difficulty. On the occasion of repeated visits I had made many and strict enquiries of the labourers employed about the spot, and of the neighbours in general, as to the discovery or existence of any ancient remains either of the buildings and their ornamental accessories, or of the instruments, utensils, or other evidences of the religious or domestic life of the olden possessors. For a long time I could obtain for my queries nothing but an uniform negative. At length one of a large body of farm servants set me upon the track of possessing myself of the rings of which mention has already been made, and eventually succeeded in recollecting that several large gravestones with illegible inscriptions had been dug up many years before—it was in 1836—from three to four feet under the surface of what is now the kitchen garden of the mansion. These after a long search I had at length the gratification of recovering. It is clear, from several previous notices,[*]

[*] See pp. 11, 27, 37, 74.

that there were two Churches appropriated to the adjacent Societies, the greater belonging to the Prioress and her Sisters, and dedicated to the Blessed Virgin and S. Nicholas, the less in the possession of the Preceptor and his Brethren. In which of them the remains thus brought to light originally found a place, or whether in the church-yard, also previously mentioned, it is now of course impossible to determine. The Priory Church, however, as I hinted in a former page, would appear to have been their most probable locality. The most ancient was a portion of an incised slab, (*see the figure*) with a few Lombardic characters all but obliterated :—

* : 𝔅𝔊 · 𝔓 * * * * * * * 𝔊𝔏𝔊 : *

The next was a fragment of the fifteenth century, commencing with **Orate pro**, immediately after which came the envious fracture that prevented all identification of it with the old worthy whose memory it was intended to immortalize. (*See the figure.*) Parts of four letters of a second line remained—**land**—no doubt the last syllable of the name of the House—thus :—

Orate pro
land

A third fragment, of the same period as the last, read

Schereb̄o
ppicietur d

The former line had its two concluding letters imperfect, but represented, perhaps, a part of the word "Schereborn;" the latter was evidently a portion of the well known formula. (*See the figure.*) There was yet another memorial, and that of a most touching character. It was the only one that was found entire, and had accordingly been taken some care of and placed in a cellar. Nothing, however, was known of it, except that it had upon it a number of old letters which nobody could read. I duly obtained leave, most courteously accorded by the tenant of the mansion, to examine the mysterious relic; and, after transporting a range of brewing utensils which were marshalled upon it, discovered at length the object of my search covered with the dust that many years during which it had been untouched had collected on its surface. This was soon removed, and I was then most amply rewarded for my labour. The object brought to light was a noble incised slab, *(see the figure)* about seven feet long by four feet broad, of thirteenth or early fourteenth century work, in commemoration, as I conjecture, of a deceased Prioress. A very beautiful Lombardic cross occupied the centre, on either side of which was one line of the inscription, almost as sharply defined as when it left the hand of the old workman:—

"Sister Alienor of Actune lies here, on whose soul God have mercy. Amen." The epitaph is slightly abbreviated from the more usual formula, but the letters are remarkably fine, and the whole is of a truly artistic character. This, however, we may consider its least interesting peculiarity. It is eloquent of something higher than even Christian art, how noble and beautiful soever. Who Sister Alienor of Actune was, although this is not forgotten elsewhere, is now, I fear, beyond the power of the genealogist to discover for us and declare. But this venerable gravestone, disinterred from its long night of centuries, has once more made the world acquainted with her name, and will now, doubtless, through her unworthy remembrancer, do so to a far wider extent than it ever transmitted it before. Such publicity will not now interfere with her repose. And that which has at length furnished so graceful a memorial of her is surpassingly worthy of reverent remark. It is a silent and yet speaking witness of one who "did what she could" in her ancient day; who, perhaps with much to discourage and distress her, laboured and fainted not in her high resolve; and at length, when human toils were over, entered into that rest for which, it cannot be too much to imagine, her life in this sacred home very eminently tended to prepare her. Nor shall I, as I hope, be considered fanciful in adding, that it may symbolize also the System with which it was connected—buried, past, and gone—yet preservative, and indeed full, of beautiful forms and holy thoughts for those who will reverently examine it and wipe away the dust that has settled upon its surface, and trace, as they so well may, its distinguishing lines, telling at once of the Cross which was its centre, the union which was its strength, and the hope of final mercy which was alike its mainstay and its reward.

APPENDIX.

No. I.

[MS. Cott. Tib. E. ix., f. 23.]

.... ANDE. Wms de Erlegh p' salute a'ic Henrici Regis et Ael . . . . sui R' Henric' & alioru' filioru' & filiaru' suaru' . . . . . conc' eis tot^am de Buckland & ecc' de Pereton' . . . . plantand' & ordinand' p' manu' Tho: Archep'i Avun . . . . . . religionem apud Buckland &^c cu' usu eccl'aru & . . . .

[MS. in Off. Armor, L. 17, f. 141.]

Anno d'nice incarnationis 1434 hunc libru' taliter co'pilauit frater Joh'es Stillingflete de no'ib' fundator' hospitalis s'ci Joh'is Jerusalem in Anglia &c.

[MS. in Off. Armor, L. 17, f. 153.]

BUKLAND. Will'ms de Erlegh p' salute ai'e Regis Henrici & Alienore Regine & filij sui Regis Henrici & alior' filior' & filiar' suar' p' remedio ai'e ip'ius Will'mi & vxoris sue dedit tota' t'ra' de Buklande & ecclia' de Perreton' cu' alijs ecclijs et t'ris suis in diu's' loc' vt pat' p' carta' inde confecta' ad plantandu' & ordinandu' p' manu' Thome archidiaconi a'uncli ip'ius Will'mi de Erlegh Religione' apud Bukland & q^d iid'm Cano'ici sic plantati et ordinati in eodem loco p'de'as t'ras & eccl'ias in vsus suos p'p'os in pura' p'petua'   elemosina' possiderent.

No. II.

[MS. Cott. Tib. E. ix., f. 23.]

Will'ms d' Erlegh p'dict' dn's de Driston dedit ad edificand' domu' de B. . . . . cu' eccl'ia de Pereton, cu' o'ib' capellis membris &c. s's ecc' de Chedscy . . . o'i iure q'd fres' he'nt in eccl'ia de Poulett cu' capella de Huntw'th & Newton Comitis & de Thurlackston & de Sirdeston & de Newton & eccl'ia de Bekynton & de Kynm'sdon & de Sirston &c.

[MS. in Coll. Armor, L. 17, f. 153b.]

Will'mus de Erlegh p'dc'us dn's de Driston dedit ad edifica'da' domu' de Bukland cu' eccl'ia Pereton cu' om'ib' membris capellis & p'tin' suis s' eccl'ia' de Chedscy q' est me'bru' eius & cu' om'i iure q^d ff'res hospital' h'nt v'l habere debebu't in eccl'ia de Poulet no'ie eccl'ie de Pereton cu' capella de Huntworth & capella de Neweton Comit' & capella de Thurlakeston & capella d' Sirdeston & capella de Neweton Regis & dedit eccl'ia' de Bekynton' cu' om'ib' p'tin' & ecclia' de Kynm'sdon ac ecclia' de Sirston cu' alijs pl'rib' t'ris & bonis.

No. III.

[MS. in Coll. Arm., L. 17, f. 155.]

Ip'e (Henricus Rex Anglie II.) ecia' confirmauit domu' de Bukland vt sorores ib'm & non alibi remanerent.

[MS. Cott. Tib. E. ix., f. 23.]

Qui tamen religiosi p' interfecc'oe cuiusd^{a}m Scenesca . . . . . ipi'us Will'i d' Erlegh dn's Henric' Rex 2 fecit eos . . . . Napoli tunc p'or hospit de S^{ti} Johis J'r'm in Angl ap . . . . . . multoru' et Anglie p'ceru' p' collocandis ib'm soror . . . . ut fr'es p'd'ci in nullo alio loco in Angl' retin' . . . . nisi in domo de Buckland.

[MS. in Coll. Armor, L. 17, f. 155.]

Quos quid'm Cano'icos postea p' plures annos p' eor' culpa & forisfactura, eo videl't quod quend^{a}m senescallu' suu' consangu'em Will'mi de Erlegh int'fesseru't [interfecerunt] dn's Rex Henricus II^a p' tunc existens fecit amoueri, et f'ri Garn'io de Neapoli tunc p'ori Hospitalis sc'i Johis Jher'^{lm} in Anglia apud London consensu Rad'i Cantuar' archei'pi & Reginald' Bathon' e'pi & multor' p'cer' Anglie tam el'icor' q^{a}m laicor' easd'm t'ras & ecclecias p' collocandis ib'm sororibus donauit ac confirmauit circa a^{os} dni Mill'mo c^m lxxx^m sub conuenco'ne videli't q^d id'm p'or seu sui successores in nulla alia domo sua in Anglia retineret sorores sui ordinus [ordinis] n' in p'dc'a domo de Bukland.

No. IV.

[MS. Coll. Tib. E. ix., f. 23.]

Que quidem sorores aliq . . . . . . in domibus p'tic'laribus &^{c} Canonicos p'dctos in . . . . prior tamen p'dict' consensu Regio decolla . . . fecit sorores . . . .

[MS. in Coll. Armor, L. 17, f. 153.]

Que quid'm sorores olim sp' suu' morabant viz apud Hamton iuxta Kyngeston apud Kerebrooke & Swynfeld & alijs loc'. Deinde frat' Garnerius p'dcus p'or de consensu regio cosd'm cano'icos tres viz in domu' hospital' p'd'ci ad petic'one' cor' suscepit et h'itu' eiusd'm hospital' tribuit & duos in p'oratu' de Tanton ac vnu' in p'oratu' de Berlith & vnu' in monast'iu' sc'i Barth'i de Smithfeld apud London Reginaldus ep'us Bathon' p'dc'us ip'is hec petentib' & obtantib' in Religione cano'icor' recipi fecit. Postmodu' vero hijs p'act' p'fatus ffrat' Garnarius p'or sorores in diu's' p'cept'ijs ordinis sui in Anglia vt p'd'cit' existentes vt p'dicit' congregari & ap^d Bukland de consensu ac volu'tate Regio necnon consensu om'i quor' int'fuit collocari fecit videl't sororem Milsante' apud Standon sororem Joh'am apud Hamton sororem Basilia' apud Kerebrooke sororem Amabiliam & sorore' Amisia' de Malketon' apud Shenegey sorore' Xpmam d' Hoggeshawe apud Hoggeshawe sorore' Petronillam apud Gosford et sororem Agnetam apud Clanefelde vt in eod'm loco de Buckland eod'm sorores & sue succ' deo inp'p'm deseruirent.

No. V.

[MS. Cott. Nero, E. VI., f. 467 b.]

Nomina Prioru' Hospitalis Sancti Joh'is Jerl'm in Anglia.

Frat' Garnarius de Neapoli erat primus Prior tempore fundaco'is Soror' domus de Bukland temp'e Regis Henrici sc'di qui congregauit sorores tunc p' diu'sa loca disp'sas ac temp'e d'ne ffine prime Priorisse ib'm que Priorissa vixit in ip'o statu lx annis. Iste erat Prior p' pl'res annos ante passionem Sc'i Thome Martiris & obijt vltimo die Augusti.

Frat' Ric'us de Turk Prior temp'e eiusdem Priorisse obijt xij^{mo} die Augusti.

Frat' Rad'us de Dyna Prior temp'e eiusdem Priorisse obijt xiij^{mo} die Maij.

Frat' Gilb'tus de Veer Prior temp'e eiusdem Priorisse dedit sororib' domus . . . Bukland c^s annue pens: exeunt. de man'io de Reynh^{a}m & obiit xiij^{mo} die Augusti.

Frat' Hugo de Alneto Prior temp'e eiusdem Priorisse obijt xxiij^o die Nouembr'.

Frat' Alanus Prior & Ep'us de Bangor temp'e eiusdem Priorisse obijt xix^o die Maij.

Frat' Rob'tus Thesaurarius Prior tempore eiusdem Priorisse obijt xxvj^{to} die Octobr'.

Frat' Terricus de Nussa ob.jt xxj^o die Decembr' anno d'ni mill'imo cc^{mo} xxxvij^{mo}.

Frat' Rob'tus de Maunby Prior obijt xiiij^o die mens' Octobr'.

Frat' Rog'us de Veer Prior dedit eccl'ie de Clerkenwell vna' de sex ydrijs in quib' Jhesus conu'tit aquam in vinu' anno d'ni mill'imo cc^{mo} lxix^o & obijt xv die ffebruar' anno d'ni mill'imo cc^{mo} lxx^o.

Frat' Petrus de Hakh^{a}m Prior tempore Regis E. primi obijt xj^o die Januar'.

Frat' Simon Botard Prior obijt iij^o die Maij.

Frat' Helyas Smethton Prior obijt xxvij die April'.

Frat' Steph'us ffulburn Prior obijt primo die Januar'.

Frat' Joseph Chauncy Prior obijt xix^o die Maij. Iste fieri fecit capellam d'ni Prioris in domo de Clerkenwell temp'e E. p'mi a conquestu.

Frat' Walterus Prior adquisiuit p'ceptorias de Quenyngton & Shenegey & plures terras & ten' & obijt **xxviij^o** [?] die Augusti.

Frat' Will's de Haunle Prior fieri fecit claustrum de Clerkenwell anno d'ni mill'imo cc^mo lxxxiiij^to et regni regis E. primi xij° et obijt iiij^to die ffebruar' anno d'ni sup^nd'co.

Frat' Ric'us Pauley Prior tempore Regis E. filij E. obijt iij° die Augusti.

Frat' Rob'tus de Dyna Prior obijt xxiiij^to die Nouembr'.

Frat' Will's Tothall Prior obijt xij° die Octobr' anno d'ni mill'imo ccc^mo xviij° lr'a d'nicalis D.

Frat' Thomas L'archier Prior obijt xxviij° die Augusti anno d'ni mill'imo ccc^mo xxix° hic dedit sororib' de Bukland xl^s' annuatim imp'p'm p'cipiend' de man'io de Hidon' p'tin' ad Templecombe.

Frat' Leonardus de Tyb'tis Prior obijt vltimo die Januar' temp'e huius bona Templarior' data sunt Hospitalarijs.

No. VI.

[MS. in Coll. Armor, L. 17, f. 148b.]

KEREBROOKE.—Matildis Comitissa de Clare vxo^r Will'i comit' de Clare ac mat' Ric'i comit' de Clare dedit ———
——— so'rib' dom' de Bukland xiij^s iiij^d solvend' annuati' p' man' p'ceptoris ib'm p'o temp'e existent' & alia pl'ra bona Hec donac'o f'ca fuit apud Westmon'. a° qui'to rr' Ric'i p'mi & a° d'ni mill'mo c' lxxxxij° & tempore ff'ris Ala' p'oris hospitalis in Anglia & Ep'i de Bangor.

No. VII.

will be found included in No. V.

No. VIII.

[MS. Cott. Tib. E. IX., f. 23.]

Deinde frater Hugo de Alneto p'or hospit p'd' consensu fr . . . . d'ne Lorette comitisse Leicestrie ad inveniend' j fre'm Capella . . . celebrantem miss^am gloriose Virginis ; s's in excambio p' ter' alijs . . . .

[MS. in Coll. Armor, L. 17, f. 153b.]

Deinde ffrat' Hugo de Alneto p'or Hospital' p'dci de co'i consensu & volluntate ffr'm capituli concessit dn'e Lorrette comitisse Leycestrie ad inveniendu' vnu' ffr'm capellanu' cotidie celebrat'um missa' gloriose virginis Maria [Marie] eccl'ia Soror' p'dcar' p' c'tis t'ris redit' alijs que p'dca comitissa contulit domui hospital' sc'i Joh'is in p'p'os vsus soror' p'dcar' de Bukland conuertend' Ita q^d p'd'ctus ffrat' capellanus nulli alij s'uic'o deputabit' n' p'p'e gloriose v'ginis minist'io in eccl'ia p'd'ca.

No. IX.

[Cart. 11 Hen. III., p. 2, m. 6.]

P' Hospital' de Bocland. Rex &c. salt'. Insp^eximus cartam Lorette quonda' Comitisse Leycestr' f'eam D'o & b'e Marie & s'co Joh'i Bapt'e & b'atis paup'ib' s'ee domus hospital' Ierosol' ad sust'ntaco'em sorror' de Bocland * * in h' uerba. Not' sit om'ib' X'pi fidelib' tam p'sentib' q^a futuris hoc script' visuris v'l audituris q'd ego Loretta comitissa Leycestr' dedi & concessi D'o & b'e Marie & sc'o Joh'i Bapt'e & b'is paup'ib' domus hospital' Ierosol' ad sust'ntaco'em soror' de Boclaund D'o s'uienciu' & ad inueniend' quendam cap'll'm fr'em in cade' domo qui cotidie & p'petuo missam in honore b'e Virginis Marie i' maiori eccl'ia ap' Bokland. ad altare b'e Virginis celebret p' salute anime mee & d'ni Rob'i viri mei Com' quonda' Leicestr' & p' salute a'iar' p'ris & m'ris mee & om'iu' ancessor' & successor' meor' tota' t'ram meam de Noteston' & totam t'ram meam de Ynesford ex^a aq^am & vlt^a aq^am & lxiiij ac^as de d'nico meo sup' Ruwedon' & totam t'ram meam de Ridescot' & de Hele & de Chorlecot' & de Tunecot'. & de Boteburn' & totam t'ram q^a tenet Philipp' at Viam cu' ho'ib' p'd'cas t'ras tenentib'. & p't'ea cent' ac^as de d'nico meo in Frem'esmore & boscu' meu' qui uocat' Anc^rwd' & vnu' ferling' ad Roitheye cu' om'ib' p'tin' suis in man'io de Toustok cu' pasturis & om'ib' aliis ad p'd'cas t'ras p'tin'tib'. Et p't'ea om'imoda' com'unam int' ten'ta mea vbiq' lib'e & * h'end' & possidend' in p'petuam & puram elemosina' sic' ulla elemos' lib'ius & quiccius dari potest. & vt h' mea donac'o futuris temp'ib' p'petue firmitatis robur optineat. eam p'sentis sc^rp' munimi'e cu' sigilli mei app'oe dign' duxi roborare. Hiis testib'. Mag'ro Lamb'to subdecano Wal'nsi d'no Philippo de Alben'. d'no Rog'o de La Cuche. Ada' fil'

Hondebrand' Mag'ro Vmfr' Canon Cycestr' Mag'ro Regin' de Mereston'. Will'o capell'o de Bukingeh'. Walt'o cl'rico de Langeh'. Thom' cl'rico de Glouccestr'. Nich' de Wyleya. & aliis. Nos hanc donat' & concessione' rata' & g^{a}tas h'entes. p'd'co hospitali & sororib' p'd'cis eam p' nob' & h'edib' n'ris concedim' & co'firmamus. T. ut sup^a Dat' ut sup^a. (Dat' p' manu' R. Cycestr' ep'i &c. ap' Westm. xvj die Jul' anno &c. xj°.)

No. X.

[MS. Cott. Tib. E. ix., f. 23.]

Rad' filius Will'mi de Bremerye dedit Sororib' p'd' ccc' de Toland. Alan' filius Ant'i Russell ccel^{a}m de Danington in dioc. Linc. Warin' de Aula, Budescombe &c.

Ascuid Musard Chiltcombe Wysang^r & Bochelcotte.

Rob'tus Arundale Halse &c.

[MS. in Coll. Armor, L. 17, f. 153b.]

Rad'us filius Will'i de Briwere dedit sororib' ib'm ecclia' de Toland cu' p'tin'.

Alanus filius Ant'i Russell dedit ecclia' de Donington in dioc' Lyncolne p'tin' eisd'm.

Warinus de Aula dedit Bodescombe p'tin' eisd'm sororibus.

Ascuid Musard dedit Chiltcombe Wysangre & Bochelcote.

Rob'tus Arundale dedit Halse c'm p'tin.

No. XI.

[Pat. 12 Hen. III., m. 2.]

P' sororib' de Bocland.—D'ns R' i'tuitu D'i co'cessit sororib' de ordine Hospital' S'ci Joh'is J'rlm ap' Bocland d'o s'uientib' & s'uit'is qd singul' sept' capiant i' p'co d'ni R' de Neuton de mortuo bosco ciusd' p'ci vna' carectatam busce ad focu' suu'. Et q' compete'tius i' estate qa' i' hyeme cape' pot'nt p'de'am busca', co'cessit eis d'ns R' q'd a Pasch' usq' ad festu' S'ci Pet' ad Vincula busca' p'dcam capiant i' p'dco p'co ad num'm carectar' q' de toto anno eis compet'nt sed'm concess' n'rum p'dcam. In cui' &c. T. R. ap. Neubir' iij die Aug'.

Et mand' Ric'o de Wrotha' qd eas p'd'cam busca' cap'e p'mittat sic' p'dc'm est. T'. ut s^a.

No. XII.

[MS. in Coll. Armor, L. 17, f. 153.]

Deinde ffrat' Terricus de Mussa p'or hospital' p'dci de concilio ffr'm gen'alis capit'li dedit d'eis sororib' de Bukland & successorib' suis xxx^{ta} & octo m^arcas duodecim solidos & octo denarios st'lingor' annuati' recipiend' inp'p'm ad duos anni t'minos viz ad f'm pasche decem & noue' ma'cas sex solidos & quatuor denarios de p'ceptore d' Bukland qui p' tempore fu'it ita q^d p'ceptor de p'dcis xxxviij ma'c' xij^s & viij^d a d'co Terrico & successoribus suis h'ebit allocac'one' sup' responc'one sua soluenda.

No. XIII.

[MS. Cott. Tib. E. ix., f. 23.]

Consequent^r fr' Rog'us de Ver p'or hospit'lis p'dict in adventu suo ad . . . . . p' statu dom' ordinavit &^c.

[MS. in Coll. Armor, L. 17, f. 153b.]

Consequent' v° ffrat' Roge'us de Ver p'or hospital' p'd'ci in aduentu suo ad Bukland p' statu domus videndo invenit distancia' & discordia' int' p'iorem p'ceptorem & p'orissa' ac conuentu' dom' de Bukland p' diu's' reb' d'cas priorissa' & sorores tangentib' et assensu capit'li sui de Melcheburn ad p'petua' pace' int' ip'os s'uanda' ordinauit int' cet'a q^d p'dc'e p'orissa & conuentus h'ebunt senescallu' suu' ad mensa' p'ceptoris & unu' garc'one' sedentem cu' garconib' p'ceptoris & erit ibi cotidie in mensa nisi dux'it h'ue s'm dicti senescalli & ad f'm sc'i Mich'is cu' tinere volu'it senescallus curia' de la hele h'ebit de selario qui'q' albos panes & costrellos suos plenos s'uicie et ad id'm f'm p' cur' de Kynm'sdon d' Primmilegh tenend' h'ebit totid'm & ad le hokeday totide' equitatura' vero & om'ia alia nece'ia h'ebit de lib'ac'oe & ordinaco'e p'orissa [p'orisse] & conuent'. Et si in aliquo deliquerit, licebit p'orisse ea' [eu'] defendere ne de bonis car' int°mittat sed non eu' remouere absq' p'ore. It'm h'ebunt saserdote' s'clarem ad celebrandu' p' ani'a Sororis ffine quond^am p'orisse ib'm & a'iab' fundator' & b'nfactor' d'ce dom' qui erit in mensa cu' ffrib' & lectu' in thalamo int' sas'dotes & cl'icos & p' relicu' tempus scd'm dispoco'ne' p'orisse ita q^d p'ceptor he'at allocaconc' de quinq' m^arer' p' mensa d'ci sacerdot' & ecia' vni' ffris celebrant' missa' bc' Marie & ecia' tres solidos ad f'm sc'i Mich'is p' cl'ico de capella.

No. XIV.

[MS. in Coll. Armor, L. 17, f. 156.]

Edwardus Rex Anglie a conquestu p'mus concessit —— vnu' mercatu' singul' sept' p' die' Lune apud Man'iu' suu' de Halse in Com' Som's.

[Cart. 18 Edw. I., m. 19, n. 80.]

P' P'ore hospitalis S'ci Joh'is Je'rlm in Angl'. R' archiep'is &c. salt'm. Sciatis nos concessisse & hac carta n'ra confirmasse dil'co nob' in X'po f'ri Will'o de Henleye Priori Hospital' S'ci Joh'is Jer'lm in Angl' q'd ipe & successores sui imp'petuu' h'eant vnum m'catum sing'lis septimanis p' diem Lune apud man'ium suu' de Hause in Com' Som's'. Nisi m'catum illud sit ad nocumentu' vicinar' m'cator'. Concessim' eciam &c. —— Quare volum' & firmit' p'cipim' p' nob' & h'edib' n'ris q'd p'dcus Prior & successores sui imp'petuu' h'eant p'd'cm m'catu' apud man'ium suu' de Hause cu' om'ib' lib'tatib' & lib'is consuetudinib' ad hui'modi m'catum p'tinentib'. Nisi &c. —— Hiis testib' ven'abilib' p'rib' G. Wygorn' R. Bathon' & Wellen. A. Dunolmens' & Th. Mencuens' Ep'is. Edmundo fr'e n'ro. Will'o de Valencia auunc'lo n'ro. Gilb'to de Clare Com' Glouc' & H'tf'. Henrico de Lacy comite Linc'. Humfrido de Bohun comite Heref' & Essex. Rog'o de Bigod comite Norf' & Marescallo Angl'. Ottone de Grandisono. Petro de Chaumpnent. Ric'o de Bosco & aliis. Dat' p' manu' n'ram apud Westm. vj die Maij.

No. XV.

will be found included in No. V.

No. XVI.

[MS. Harl. 6965, p. 17.]

Official. Cur. Cant. dicreto viro mag'ro Ric'o de Thistelden officiali d'ni Radulphi ep'i Bath. & Well. salut. Ex parte religiosorum viroru' Prioris & fr'um Hosp. sci Joh. Jer'lm in Angl. nobis extitit intimatum q^d cu' vos pretenderetis prefatos religiosos ad exhibendu' titulu' si quem haberent in ecc'lis de Northpederton, Durston, Halse, Bromfild, & Kynemersden, Bath. & Well. dioc. quas in usus proprios canonici possidebant, & possiderant ab antiquo, & ad prestand' vener. p'ri pred'co obedientiam rac'oe eccli'aru' pred'carum coram vobis d'ci p'ris commissario speciali ad judiciu' evocatos pars eorundem religiosoru' cora' vobis in judiciu' sufficienter comparens, ut sibi copiam commissionis & certificatorij citaco'is p' vos in hac parte pretensarum fieri faceretis, a vobis cum instantia debita postulavit, sed vos —— effectualiter exaudire, aut copiam hujusmodi eidem facere non curastis, sed d'cos religiosos contumaces, cu' non essent, pronunciastis, ipsosq' —— in immoderata pecunie summa mulctastis, ipsamq' mulctam a preceptore f'ribus & sororibus domus d'eorum religiosoru' de Boclaunde d'ce dioc. levanda' fieri decrevistis & levari mandastis &c. appellatu' ad sede' Ap'licam, —— quare vobis inhibemus —— ne pendente in Cur. Cant. hujusmodi negotio quicquam hac occasione in d'ce partis appellantis prejudiciu' attemptetis &c. dat. Lond. 6 Kal. Oct. [1329.]

No. XVII.

[MS. in Coll. Armor, L. 17, f. 156b.]

Henric' Rex Anglie iij' [iiij'] ampliauit & pleniu' declarauit carta' q^{a}m Henric' Rex Anglie p'genitor suus concessit p'orisse & sororib' demus de Bukeland videli't q^d ip'e quali't septi'ana imp'p'm cap'ent in p'co suo de Pederton tres carectatas busce p' focali suo & ista v'ba tres carectatas

PRIORY AND PRECEPTORY. 101

busce de spinis alno & arabil' ad focu' suu' & postea
inveniab't' q^d p'd'ce p'orissa & sorores non erant capaces
d'ce concessionis eo q^d sunt obedienciare P'oris Hospital'
S'ci Joh'is Jher'lm in Anglia i'o custodes d'ni Regis i'bm
d'eam concessione' h'ere non p'misit. Quare Rex Henric'
qⁿrtus p'd'ens de gra' sp'ali a⁰ sui x⁰ concessit p' salute a'ie
sue ac Joh'ne consort' sue n^cnon Maria [Marie] consort'
sue defuncte q^d p'or Hospital' & succ' sui imp'p'm p' se &
s'uient' suos de Buk' p'cipiant quali't septi'ana iij carectatas
subbosci infra p'cu' suu' de Pederton viz Thorn aller mapell
& hasell ad vsum & p'ficuu' d'car' P'orisse & soror' & succ'
suar' imp'p'm. Et q^d queli't carectata subbosci p'd'ci
existat de tractu sex equor' & q^d ip'i p'st'nant succidant &
carient ad voluntate' sua' subboscu' p'dcu' quol't a⁰ a festo
An'unc' be' Marie vsq' f'm Omi' Scor' q^d antea erat
concess' eis a Pasca vsq' f'm S'ci Petri ad uincula
absq' impedimento seu p'turbac'one aliquali officiarior'
d'ni Regis.

[Pat. 10 Hen. IV., p. 1, m. 19.]

P" Priorissa & sororib' de Bueland. R' om'ib' ad quos
&c. sal'tm. Sciatis q'd cum dil'ce nob' in Xpo Priorissa
& sorores ordinis hospitalis S'ci Joh'is Jer'lm de Bueland
nobis monstrau'int qualit' nobilis p'genitor n'r Henr' nup'
Rex Angl' p' cartam suam quam confirmauim' concessit
sororib' domus p'dce tunc deo s'uientib' & s'uituris qd ip'e
quali't septimana imp'pm cap'ent in parco suo de Perton
iam vocato Pederton tres carectatas busce p' focali suo p'
ista v'ba tres carectatas busce de spinis alno & arabl' ad
focum suu' ac p' eo qd competencius extitit ad capiend'
buscam p'deam in estate q^am in yeme concessit eis qd ip'e
cap'ent buscam p'deam in parco p'dco a Pascha vsq' festum
S'ci Petri ad vincula ad num'u' carectar' que eis de toto
anno p'tinerent iuxta concessionem p'deam p'ut in carta &
confirmac'oe p'deis plenius continet' qd q' vigore concessionis & confirmac'ois p'dear' p'fate Priorissa & sorores in
pacifica omn' p'dear' carectar' busce infra parcum p'dem
annuatim p'ut in concessione & confirmac'oe p'deis fit
mencio a tempore confecco'is car'dem extiterunt absq'
aliquo impedimento seu g^auamine n'ri vel p'genitor' n'ror'
p'deor' aut custodum parei p'dei qui p' tempore fuerunt
seu alior' ministror' vel officiarior' ibidem quor'cumq'

quousq' iam tarde q'd nunc custos n'r ibidem ipas buscam p'dcam aut aliquam parcellam ciusdem iuxta concessionem & confirmacoem p'dcas h'cre non p'misit p' eo qd p'dcc Priorissa & sorores sunt obedienciarie Priori hospitalis S'ci Joh'is Jer'lm in Angl' ac qd ip'c p'sone capaces p'ut p'dcus custos sup' ip'as imponit non existunt. Vnde nob' supplicarunt sibi p' nos de gra' & remedio in hac parte p'uideri. Nos de gra' n'ra sp'ali & ad effc'm qd p'dce Priorisa & sorores p' salubri statu n'ro ac carissime consortis n're Johanne dum vixim' & p' a'iab' n'ris cum ab hac luce mig^au'im' necnon p' a'ia carissime consortis n're Marie defuncte denocius exorent & qd om'imoda ambiguitas & dubia hui' v'bor' de spinis alno & arabl' in concessione p'dca specificator' amoucant' concessim' p' nobis & heredib' n'ris quantum in nob' est Walt'o Grendon Priori d'ci hospitalis S'ci Joh'is Jerl'm in Angl' & successorib' suis impp'm qd ip'c & successores sui p' se & s'uientes suos d'ci hospitalis de Bucland h'eant & p'cipiant quali't septimana tres carectatas subbosci infra boscum n'rm p'dcm siue Parcum de Pederton videl't thorn aller mapel & basell ad vsum & p'ficuu' p'dcar' Priorisse & soror' & successor' suar' impp'm et q'd quel't carectata subbosci p'dci de tractu sex equor' existit q'dq' p'fatus Prior & successores sui p'dci vel s'uientes sui p'dci h'eant & p'cipiant p'dcas tres carectatas subbosci vt p'dcm est impp'm & qd ip'i p'sternant succidant & carient ad voluntatem suam subboscum p'dcm p' focali p'dcar' Priorisse & soror' & successor' suar' quol't anno a festo Anunciaco'is b'e Marie vsq' festum O'im Scor' ad num'u' carectar' que cis aut successorib' suis p' totu' annu' p'tinebunt absq' p't'baco'e impedimento seu g^uuamine n'ri vel heredum n'ror' aut Custodis n'ri d'ci bosci n'ri vel parci seu alt'ius officiarij siue ministri n'ri vel heredum n'ror quor'cumq'. In cuius &c. T. R. apud West'm xiiij die Nouemb'i. p' b're de priuato sig'.

No. XVIII.

[MS. Lansd. 200, ff. lxxxiiii, lxxxiiii b.]

ASSEMBLIA tent' in domo de Clerkenwel xx die Januarij, 1500, P'ntib' ib'm p'sonal'r R^{do} d. p'ori ffr' Jo. Kendal. ff. H.

Hawley. ff. B. Pek. ff. Ro. Dauson. ff. T. Newport. ff. Ro. Danyel. ff. A. Chetwod. ff. Jo. Tonge. ff. Jo. Bowth. & ffr. Will'o Darel P'ceptrib'—

OM'IB' X'pi fidelibus ad quos p'sens scriptum Indentatum peruen'it ffrater Joh'es Kendall Prior Hospit'lis Sancti Joh'is J'rlm in Anglia Et ciusdem P'oris Conf'res Salt'm in d'no sempit'na'. SCIATIS nos p'fatos Priorem & conf'res vna'mi nostris assensu et consensu tradidisse et ad firma' dimisisse Joh'i Vernay de ffarefelde in Com' Som's' armigero preceptoria' n'ram de Buclande Prioris in dicto Com' cu' manerijs de Bodmescomb et Cove in Com' Deuon' eidem p'ceptoric p'tinentib' et cu' om'ib' et sing'lis alijs dominijs t'ris et ten'tis pratis pascuis et pasturis redditib' et s'uicijs conf'rijs in Com' Som's' & Deuon' curijs cu' car' p'ficujs decimis oblaco'ib' bonis et catallis felonu' et fugitinor' et cu' om'ib' alijs libertatib' emolimentis et com'oditatib' quibuscuq' ad d'cam p'ceptoria' qualit'cumq' spectantib' et p'tinentib' Boscis & subboscis aduocac'onib' Eccl'iar' wardis maritagijs & releuijs duntaxat exceptis Ac nobis p'fato Priori et succ' n'ris om'ino res'uat' HABEND' & tenend' predicta' p'ceptoria' cu' om'ib' suis p'tinen' p'dict' except' p'except' p'fato Joh'i Vernay et assignatis suis a festo Natiuitatis Sc'i Joh'is Bap^{te} prox' futur' post data' p'sens' vsq' ad fine' et term' Triginta annor' extu'c p'x' sequens et plenarie complendor' REDDENDO inde an^{tim} nobis p'fato P'ori et succ' n'ris apud thesauria' n'ram de Clerkenwell p'pe London Nonaginta et tres libras sex solidos & octo denarios sterlingor' ad festa Purificaco'is b'te Marie Virginis et S'ci Barnabe ap'li equis porc'onib' durante termi'o p'dicto IT'M p'dictus ffirmarius et assignati sui sumptib' suis p'prijs tenebu't debita' et honesta' hospitalitatem infra dicta' p'ceptoria' Necno' sumptib' suis inuenient sed'm antiqua' consuetudine' quinq' Capellanos videlic' duos Capellanos de cruce vel alios duos quos nos p'dictus Prior vel succ' n'ri deputabimus infra Eccl'iam de Buclande priorissa vnu' Capellanu' infra capella' p'ceptoric ib'm vnu' Capellanu' apud Bodmescomb' et vnu' Capellanu' apud Durston diuina continuo ib'm celebraturos durante termi'o p'dicto Necnon victu' et camera' pro vno Cap^{o} d'ce priorisse atq' victu' pro seniscallo domus ciusd'm Priorisse et p' famulo suo cu' duob' bigat' feni an^{tim} eod'm termi'o durante Prouiso semp' q' dictus ffirmarius et assignati sui dabunt et soluent an^{ti}' durante dicto termi'o d'no Alexandro Vernay capellano celebranti apud Bodmescomb' camera' cu' focali suo ib'm et octo marcas sterlingor' no'ic stipendij sui et pro victu et vestitu suo sc'dm tenore' carte sub sigillo n'ro com'j cid'm d'no Alexandro facte pro termi'o vite sue. IT'M p'dictus firmarius et assignati sui soluent priorisse et Con^{tui} de Bucland p'dict' an^{tim} p' pensione sua consueta xxij^{li} atq' seniscallo curiar' dicte p'ceptorie p'tinenciu' feodu' suu' Necnon om'ia alia on'a ordinaria et extraordinaria dicte preceptorie incumbencia & imponenda p'dictus ffirmarius et assign' sui supportabu't sumptib' suis durante termi'o p'de'o Responsionib' et alijs subsidijs pro com'j thez^o Rhodi impositis et imponendis du'taxat exceptis REPARABUNT q' dictus firmarius et assign' sui om'ia domos et edificia muros sepes clausuras et fossatas dicte p'ceptorie p'tinen' durante termi'o predicto eaq' om'ia et sing'la in fine ciusd'm term'i nobis p'fato Priori & succ' n'ris in adeo bono statu quo ea recepit sursum reddent et liberabunt P'uiso q' si contingat aliqua edificia dicte p'ceptorie ad terra' propt' cor' ruinam cadere infra de'm term' In tali casu nos p'dictus Prior et succ' n'ri edificia illa nostris su'ptib' de nouo edificabim' illaq' sic de nouo edificata p'dictus ffirmarius & assignati sui cor' sumptib' postmodu' reparabu't et manutenebu't durante termi'o p'dicto IT'M dictus firmarius et assign' sui expensas mi'stror' nostri p'dicti Prioris et succ' n'ror' cu' quinq' vel sex equis veniencin' bis p' annu' ad sup'vidend' d'cam p'ceptoria' vel ad tenend' curias ib'm vel ad renouand' rentalia et alias evidencias per tres vel quatuor dies et tot noctes supportare tenca't^r durante termi'o p'dicto HABEBUNT q' dictus ffirmarius et assign' sui housebote ffyrebote ploughbote cartbote hedgebote harobote et ffoldebote in et de boscis ac subboscis dicte p'ceptorie p'tinentib' p' assignaco'em mi'stror' nostri p'dicti P'oris et succ' nostror' capiend' et in dicta p'ceptoria rac'onabilit' et sine vasto expendend' durante termi'o p'dicto ET BENE liceb^t nobis p'dicto Priori et succ' atq' mi'stris n'ris quando nobis placu'it sup'videre dicta' p'ceptoria' nostra' cu' suis p'tinen' Necnon tene' curias et face' rent'lia atq' territoria terrar' et ten'tor' p'dicte preceptorie durante termi'o p'dicto Prouiso q' dictus ffirmarius et assign' sui habebu't et p'cipie't p'ficua d'car' Curiar' cod'm termi'o durante dictus q' ffirmarius et assignati sui liberabu't nobis p'd'co Priori et succ' n'ris in fine d'ci term'j om'es rotulos curiar' et rentalia tam antiqua q^am noua que p'uenient ad manus suas durante termi'o p'dicto PROUISO semp' q' non licebit p'dicto Joh'i Vernay statum quem habet in p'dicta p'ceptoria alicui alteri dimittere sine lice'cia nostri p'dicti P'oris et succ' n'ror' durante termi'o p'dicto ET SI CON-TINGAT dictu' an'uale' redditu' lxxxxiij^{li} vj^s viij^d sterlingor' a retro fore in parte vel in toto et non solut' post aliquem terminu' soluco'is sup'ius specificatu' per duos menses Tunc bene licebit nobis predicto Priori et succ' n'ris in p'dicta' p'ceptoria' cu' suis jurib' et pertinen' vniu's' reintrare eaq' om'ia et sing'la vt in pristino statu n'ro retin'e p'nti dimissione in aliquo non obstante PROUISO semp' q' cu' p'ficua Confratriar' que sunt parcelle reuencionu' dicte p'ceptorie extimantur ad annuale' valore' lxxxxij^{li}: Idcirco si contingat &^{m} dn'm n'r'm papa' modernu' siue success' suos suspend'e dictas confr'ias aliquo tempore durante termi'o p'ntis indent^{e}e Tunc p'dictus Joh'es Vernay ffirmarius et assign' sui durante illa suspenc'one non erunt onerati cu' dicta integra annuali firma lxxxxiij^{li} vj^s viij^d sed du'taxat erunt computabiles sup' cor' sacramentu' p'dicto Priori et succ' suis de tantis pecunijs quas recipient ex nuncijs confr'iar' p'dictar' pro dictis confr'ijs et de illis du'taxat pecunijs facient soluc'onem p'dicto Priori & succ' suis dura'te suspencione p'dicta atq' de residuo pecuniar' carente ex dicta su'ma lxxxxij^{li} pro confr'ijs idem ffirmarius et assign' sui allocac'onem habebu't in p'dicta eor' annuali firma Nonaginta et triu' librar' sex solidor' et octo denarior' durante suspenco'e p'dicta ET AD OM'ES et sing'las conuenco'es p'dictas ex parte p'dicti Joh'is Vernay ffirmarij et assign' suor' cu' eff'tu p'implendas idem Joh'es Vernay obligat se heredes et executores suos p'dicto Priori & succ' suis In ducentis libris sterlingor' p' p'sentes IN CUIUS Rei testi'om tam sigillu' n'r'm co'e q'm sigillu' p'dicti Joh'is Vernay p'ntib' indenturis alt'nati' sunt appensa DAT' in domo n'ra de Clerkenwell prope London in Assemblia n'ra tent' ib'm vicesimo die Januarij a° d'ni Mill'mo Quingentesimo PROUISO semp' q' dictus ffirmarius et assign' sui in ffine p'dicti term'i dimittent et liberabu't preceptori de Buclande p'dict' p' tempore existen' om'ia orname'ta capelle ib'm siin'l cu' to° stauro viuo & mortuo specificato in dorso p'nt' indenture Dat' ut sup^a.

No. XIX.

[Miscell. Books, Off. Aug., vol. 245., no. 128.]

BUKELOND.—Here ffoloweth the yerely pencons or anuyties grauntyd by the Kinges highnes to the late P'ores and Nunes of the late surrendryd howse of Buckelonde in the countie of Som'sett. And they and eu'y of them to haue there halfe yeres penc'on at th'anuncac'on of o^r ladye next cumyng whiche shalbe in the yere of o^r lorde god a thowsande fyve hundreth xxxix, and soo from halfe yere to halfe yere during there lyves and the lyfe of eu'y of them—

That is to say

Ffurst to Katheryn Bowser p'oresse for her yerely penc'on	l^{li}
To Margaret Sydnam supp'ores	iiij^{li} xiij^s iiij^d
To Julyan Kendall	iiij^{li} vj^s viij^d
To Jone Hyll	iiij^{li}
To Anne Plumm'	iiij^{li}
To Tomysyn Huntyngton	iiij^{li}
To Katheryn Poph^{a}m	iiij^{li}
To Anne Maunsell	iiij^{li}
To Mary Dodyngton	iiij^{li}
To Ales Emerforde	iiij^{li}
To Jane Babyngton	iiij^{li}
To Mary Mathew	iiij^{li}
To Agnes Mathew	iiij^{li}
To Isabell Grene	iiij^{li}
To S's Will^{a}m Mawdesley co'fessor and p'fessyd in there order	iiij^{li}
Sm^a of the yerely pensions	cviij^{li}

Jo. Tregonwell.
William Petre.

No. XX.

[Card. Pole's Pension Book, fol. xxix.]

ffeod' { Alex'i Popham capitl' Sen^{li} ib'm p' script' Abb'is et Conven' p' a' } ç^a

PRIORY AND PRECEPTORY. 107

Buckeland
nup' monast'iu'
- An^t
  - Sup'd'ci Alex'i Popham
    p' annu' .. vj^{li} xiij^s iiij^d
  - Joh'nis Tregonwell p'
    annu' .. iiij^{li}
  - Will'i Portema' mil'
    p' annu' .. xxvj^s viij^d
  - Joh'nis Butler p' annu' xiij^s iiij^d
- Penc'
  - Johanne Hille p' annu' iiij^{li}
  - Thomasine Huntingdon p'
    annu' .. .. iiij^{li}
  - Kat'ine Pophame p' annu' iiij^{li}
  - Anne Maundefeld p' annu' iiij^{li}
  - Johanne Bavington p' annu' iiij^{li}
  - Elisabeth Grene p' annu' iiij^{li}
  - Agnes Mathewe p' annu' iiij^{li}
  - Will'i Maudesley cl'ic' p'
    annu' .. .. iiij^{li}

No. XXI.
[Abstract of Orig. 36 Hen. VIII., p. 1, r. xxxviii.]

P' Comite
Essex Jacobo Rokeby
Will'o Ibgrabe Joh'e
Cokke Edwardo Rogers
& Edwardo Bury sibi &
hered'.

Rex om'ib' ad quos &c.
salt'm Sciatis q'd nos p' sum'a
mille quadraginta nouem librar'
vndecim solidor' duor' denarior'
& vnius oboli legalis monete
Angl' ad manus &c. ——— p'
p'dil'c'm & fidelem consangui-
neu' & consiliariu' n'r'm Comi-
tem Essex ac p' dil'cos nob' Jacobum Rokeby armig'um
Will'm Ibgrabe armig'um Joh'em Cokke Edwardum Rogers
et Edwardum Bury armig'os ——— totam domu' &
Scitum nup' monast'ij de Buckland in Com' n'ro Som's'
modo dissoluto ac om'ia terr' prata pasturas & hereditamenta n'ra vocat' seu cognit' p' nomen vel p' no'i'a de
fouretene acres Newland Purches Staplehayes Roden
Lobbis Harys Horlocke Meade Hurte Meade Longe
Meade & Sixe acres Meade seu quocumq' alio no'i'e aut
quibuscumq' aliis no'ib' sciant^r censeant^r vel cognoscant^r
cum om'ib' car' p'tin' modo vel nup' in tenura siue occu-

paco'e d'ci Edwardi Rogers vel assign' suor' iaccn' & existen' in Bucklande alias dict' Buckland Soror' in d'co Com' Som's' d'co nup' Monast'io de Buckland dudum spectan' vel p'tinen' ac parcell' possessionu' inde existen' ac in manib' cultura & occupaco'e p'pria nup' Priorisse illius nup' Monast'ij de Buckland tempore dissoluco'is eiusdem nup' Monast'ij reseruat' existen' Ac om'es illos boscos n'ros & t'ras n'ras vocat' Riden Coppes & Wynsell Wood continen' p' estimaco'em decem acras cum cor' p'tin' vniu'sis in Buckland ——— Necnon om'ia domos edificia horrea stabula columbaria ortos pomaria gardina t'ram & solum n'ra quecumq' infra Scitum Septum ambitum circuitum & p'cinctum d'ci nup' Monast'ij de Buckland existen' ac om'ia & singula co'ias vias semitas casiamenta com'oditates p'ficua & emolumenta quecumq' in Buckland et Mighelchurche & Northpetherton p'dict' dict' t'ris pratis & pasturis in Buckland & Mighelchurche p'dict' quoquo modo spectan' vel p'tinen' & cum eisdem vsitat' seu occupat' existen' Acceiam totam illam Rectoriam n'ram & eccl'iam n'ram siue Capellam n'ram de Mighelchurche cum p'tin' in d'co Com' n'ro Som's' d'co nup' Monast'io de Buckland dudum spectan' & p'tinen' Necnon om'es & om'imod' decimas blador' garbar' g^{n}nor' feni lane & agnellor' ac alias decimas minutas ac oblaco'es obuenco'es & p'ficua quecumq' in Mighelchurche & Buckland p'd'cis & alibi vbicumq' d'ce Rectorie et eccl'ie siue Capelle de Mighelchurche quoquo modo spectan' vel p'tinen' ———
Et que quidem Scitus d'ci nup' Monast'ij de Buckland ac p'dict' terr' prata pascue pastur' decime ac cet'a p'missa in Buckland Northpetherton & Michelchurche p'd'cis modo extendunt^r ad clar' annuu' valorem septuaginta quinq' solidor' & octo denarior' ——— H'end' &c. in capite p' s'uiciu' vicesime partis vnius feodi militis ac reddendo annuatim &c. ——— pro p'd'cis t'ris ten' pratis pascuis pasturis rectoria decimis & cet'is p'missis in Buckland & Mighelchurche p'dict' septem solidos & septem denarios sterlingor' ——— ad festum S'ci Mich'is Arch'i singulis annis soluend' ——— Ac p't'q^{a}m de Centum sex solidis & octo denarijs annuatim soluend' p' stipendio Curat' diuina celebrant' in eccl'ia siue Capella de Mighelchurche p'dict' ——— In cuius &c. T. R. apud Westm' xxx die Junij.

No. XXII.

[Abstract of Orig. 36 Hen. VIII., p. 3, rot. xij.]

Rex om'ib' ad quos &c. salt'm Sciatis q' nos p' su'ma septingentar' quinquaginta quatuor librar' septendecim solidor' & octo denarior' bone & legalis monete n're Anglie —— Will'm Porteman s'uientem n'r'm ad legem & Alexandrum Poph^am armig'm p' manib' bene & fidelit' solut' de quaquidem sum'a septigentar' &c —— totum illud maniu' n'r'm de Northpetherton alias Northpederton in Com' n'ro Som's' cum om'ib' & singulis suis iurib' membr' & p'tin' uniu'sis nup' Prioratui de Bukland in de'o Com' n'ro Som's' modo dissolut' dudum spectan' & p'tinen' ac parcell' possessionu' reuencionu' seu p'ficuor' inde existen' ac totum situm eiusdem man'ij ac om'ia t'ras d'nicales prata pascua & pastur' cum suis p'tin' eidem man'io p'tin' seu spectan' Acetiam totum illum boscum n'r'm vulgarit' vocat' Barwoode iacen' & existen' in Northpetherton alias Northpederton p'd'ca continen' p' estimac'oem octo acras t're & bosci cum p'tin' Necnon om'ia illa mesuagia t'ras & ten' prata pascua & pastur' n'ra cum suis p'tin' iacen' & existen' in Gotton infra parochiam de Westemonketon in d'co Com' n'ro Som's' d'co nup' prioratui Bukeland dudum spectan' & pertinen' —— in tenuris siue occupaco'ib' Ric'i Warr Armig' Rob'ti Warr Will'i Hare & Weltheane Merkes vidue —— Necnon om'ia mesuagia tofta domos edificia orrea stabula columbaria molendina ortos gardina pom'ia t'ras ten' prata &c. —— boscos subboscos —— aquas stagna viuaria gurgites — piscaco'es, co'ias, vasta &c—feod'milit' &c—in Northpetherton alias Northpederton Michelchurche Bromfeld Brymton Raiff Wollauington & Mirelinche ac in Gotton in d'ca parochia de Westmonekton — aut alib' vbicunq' in eodem Com' n'ro Som's' —— Necnon mesuag' &c —— in Ayshe & Thornfaycon in d'co Com' n'ro Som's' —— Necnon vnu' ten' & mesuagiu' n'r'm cum suis p'tin' iacen' & existen' in parochia de Bromefeld in d'co Com' n'ro Som's' nup' prioratui de Taunton in d'co Com' n'ro Som's' modo dissolut' dudum spectan' & p'tinen' &c —— Acetiam aliud mesuagiu' in Bromefeld modo in tenura seu occupaco'e cuiusdam Joh'is Pylman —— Necnon terr' in Kyngeshyll in parochia de Spaxton in d'co Com' n'ro Som's' d'co nup' prioratui de Taunton dudum spectan' &c —— Insup' totum illud man'iu' firmam & grang' n'ra' de Claveshey cum p'tin' in parochijs de Northepetherton & Bromefelde p'd'cis Necnon totum illud Capitale mesuagiu' domum situm & capitalem mancionem man'ij firme & grangie n'ror' de Claveshey p'd'ca modo siue nup' in tenura siue dimissione d'ci Will'i Portman vel assign' suor' nup' monast'io de Athelney in d'co Com' n'ro Som's modo dissolut' dudum spectan' & pertinen' Necnon boscum n'r'm vulgarit' vocat' Chalveshey Wood continen' p' estimaco'em decem acras t're & bosci ac boscum n'r'm vocat' Holesey Wood continen' p' estimaco'em quinq' acras t're & bosci iacen' & existen' in Northepetherton p'd'ca cum p'tin' d'co nup' monast'io de Athelney p'tinen' & spectan' —— Necnon om'ia & singula domos &c d'co man'io firme & grangie aliquo modo spectan' &c. Quequidem in Northepetherton Michelchurche Bromfeld Brymton Raiff Wollauington Mirelinche & Gotton d'co nup' Prioratui de Bucland dudum spectan' & p'tinen' sunt clari annui valoris viginti triu' librar' septemdecim solidor' & quatuor denarior' —— Ac quequidem in Ayshe & Thornefaveon sunt clari annui valoris quadraginta septem solidor' & sex denar' —— Et quequidem in Bromefeld & Spaxton —— quadraginta vnius solidor' & octo denar' —— Et quequidem maner' &c. de Claveshey —— nouem librar' —— Reddend' annuatim —— p' Northepetherton &c. triginta octo solidos —— p' Gotton nouem solidos vnu' denariu' & vnu' obulum —— p' Ayshe & Thornfaveon quatuor solidos & nouem denarios —— p' Bromefeld & Spaxton quatuor solidos & duos denarios —— p' Claveshey octodecim solidos In cujus rei &c. T. R. apud Westm' xiij die Octobr'.

No. XXIII.

[Abstract of Orig. 36 Hen. VIII., p. 8, rot. xvii.]

Rex om'ib' ad quos &c. salt'm. Sciatis qd nos p' sum'a nonnigentar' nonaginta nouem librar' sexdecim solidor' & septem denarior' legalis monete Angl' &c. p' Alex'm Popham armig'um & Will'm Halley gen'osum —— totum illud man'iu' & totam illam nup' Preceptoriam n'ram de Bucklond Pryours in Com' n'ro Som's' cum man'io de Halse ac om'ib' alijs man'ijs t'ris tentis p*tis pascuis pasturis

redditib' reu'sionib' s'uicijs & cet'is hereditamentis quibuscumq' iacen' & existen' in d'co Com' n'ro Som's' d'ce nup' P'ceptorie de Buckelond Priours p'tin' cum om'ib' alijs suis iurib' membris & p'tin' vniu'sis —— modo vel nup' in tenura dimissione siue occupaco'e p'fati Will'i Halley vel assign' suor' Necnon Rectoriam & eccl'iam imp'priatam de Halse ac om'es & singulas alias Rectorias & eccl'ias imp'priat' n'ras d'ce Preceptorie p'tinen' ac om'es glebas decimas penciones porco'es oblaco'es obuenco'es fruct' commoditates p'ficua emolumenta & hereditamenta n'ra quecumq' tam spiritualia q^m temporalia cuiuscumq' sint gen'is —— necnon aduocaco'es & iura pr'onat' Rectoriar' & eccl'iar' p'dict'. Ac etiam om'ia illa duo man'ia n'ra de Bodmescombe & Cove in Com' n'ro Deuon' cum om'ib' &c.——
Necnon aduocaco'es donaco'es p'sentaco'es &c. eccl'ie & Rectorie de Hethefeld & eccl'ie & R'torie de Halse ——
Necnon totum illum boscum & grouam n'ram voc' Wynsell Groue continen' p' estimaco'em quatuor acras t're & bosci ac totam illam boscum & grouam n'ram vocat' Peryfeld Groue continen' p' estimaco'em quatuor acras t're & bosci ac totam illam grouam n'ram vocat' Bowyers Grove continen' p' estimaco'em duodecim acras bosci & vasti ac totum illum boscum & vastum n'r'm vocat' Bodmescombe Wood continen' p' estimaco'em triginta quinq' acras bosci & vasti necnon duodecim acras t're ac sexdecim acras t're & viginti septem acras t're vocat' Vprynges of Wood —— parcell' d'ce nup' P'ceptorie de Bucklond Pryours —— Insuper dominiu' & man'iu' de Thurlebare &c. nup' Prioratui de Taunton spectan' &c. ——
Ac mesuagiu' &c. vocat' Playstrete &c. nup' Prioratui de Taunton &c. Ac redditum viginti & quatuor solid' nouem denar' & vnius obuli vocat' le Thurchetts exeun'de quibusdam t'ris &c. in Thurlebare —— Et vnu' clausum bosci vocat' le Pryours Wood continen' tresdecim acras bosci ——
Necnon totum maneriu' & dominiu' n'r'm de Tobrydge cum om'ib' suis iurib' &c. in parochia S'ci Jacobi iuxta Taunton Prioratui de Taunton spectan' &c.——Que quid'm man'iu' & nup' Preceptoria de Buckelond Priours vna cum d'co man'io de Halse ac om'ib' alijs man'ijs &c. sunt de claro annuo valore triginta vnius librar' nouemdecim solidor' & duor' denarior' decima inde nob' p' p'sentes reseruat' non deduct' et que quidem vicaria est de claro annuo valore quinq'

librar' nouemdecim solidor' quinque denarior' & vnius obuli decima inde nob' res'uata non deducta. Et que quidem Rectoria de Hethefeld &c. nouem librar' & quatuor solidor' decima inde &c. reseruat' non deduct'——P'ceptoriam de Bucklond Pryours ac Halse tenend' in capite p' s'uiciu' militare videl't p' vicesimam partem vnius feodi militis, ac reddend' &c. p' Buckelond & Halse tres libras tres solidos & vndecim denarios bone & legalis monete n're Angl'—— p' Tobrydge decem solidos & septem denarios——p' Thurlebare quatuordecim solidos & quinq' denarios —— ad festum S'ci Mich'is Arch'i singulis annis soluend' —— In cuius rei &c. T. R. apud Westm' xvj die ffebruarij anno R. sui tricesimo sexto.

No. XXIV.

[Abstract of Orig. 2 Edw. VI., p. 1, r. xlv.]

Rex om'ib' ad quos &c. salt'm Sciatis &c. p' sex libris tresdecim solidis & quatuor denarijs &c. —— concessim' dil'co nob' Will'o Halley gen'oso q'd ipse unu' capitale mesuagiu' suu' vocat' Buckelond Priors cum p'tin' ac duo gardina duo pomaria ducentas acras t're triginta sex acras prati sexaginta tresdecim acras pasture & duas acras t're aque coop'tas cum p'tin' in Buckland Priors & Coglod in Com' Som's' que de nob' tenent' in capite ut dicit' dare possit & concedere alienare confirmare aut cognosc'e p' finem in Cur' n'ra &c. dil'cis nob' Joh'i Cuffe & Joh'i Tynbery h'end' & tenend' sibi & hered' suis &c. Et eisdem Joh'i & Joh'i &c. de p'fato Will'o recip'e possint & ten'e &c. similit' licenciam dedim' ac dam' sp'alem Et vlt'ius concessim' &c. p'fatis Joh'i & Joh'i q'd ip'i Capitale mesuagiu' p'd'em ac om'ia & singula p'missa cum p'tin' dare concedere & recognosc'e possint p'fato Will'o & Margarete vx'i cius h'end' & tenend' eisdem Will'o & Margareta ac hered' &c. licenciam dedim' & dam' sp'alem —— In cujus &c. T. R. apud Westm' xiij die Februarij.

T. H.

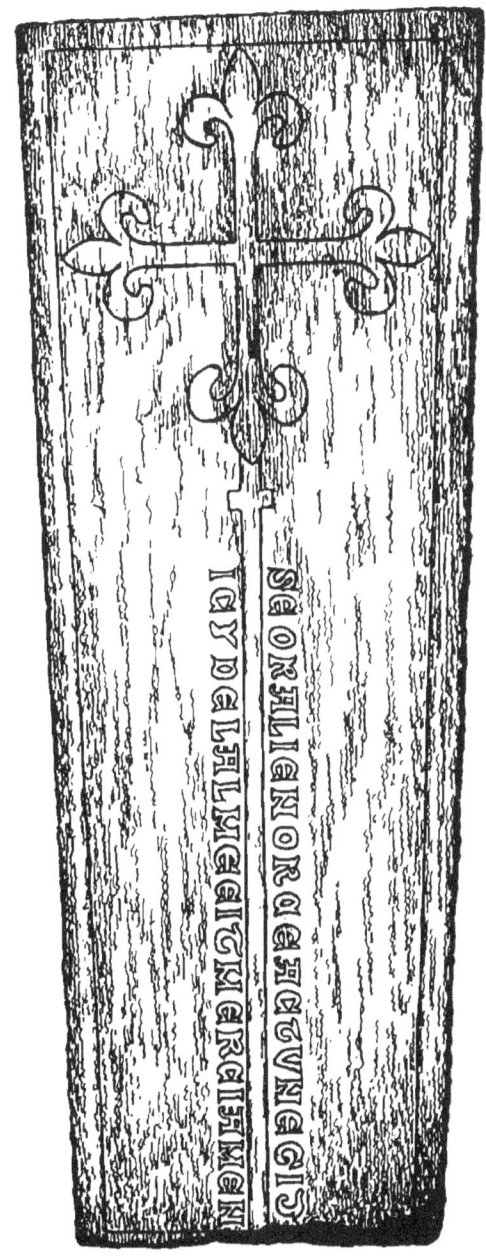

FROM MYNCHIN BUCKLAND PRIORY.

Tho. Hugo del. & lith. 1861.

RINGS FOUND NEAR THE SITE OF MYNCHIN BUCKLAND PRIORY.

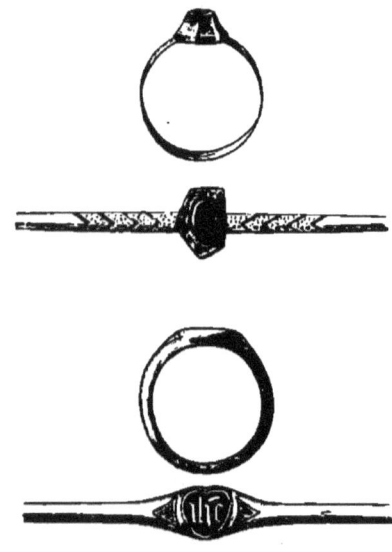

(*Actual Size.*)

Drawn and Engraved for the Rev. Thomas Hugo's History of Buckland Priory.

www.ingramcontent.com/pod-product-compliance
Lightning Source LLC
Chambersburg PA
CBHW021941160426
43195CB00011B/1186